To: Tamara

Thank

so hospitable. I look
forward to a great
friendship.

Chuck

MW00654885

Exposed

Dr. Chuck McAlister

Promise of Hope Ministries
Chattanooga, Tennessee

Acknowledgements

This book is the result of a team effort. In fact, without the assistance of an unselfish group of people, it would never have happened.

To my family, thank you for the Christian legacy that you have given me. My prayer is that I will be found faithful as I follow your example.

To my sons, Chris and Jeff, and to Brandi, Chris' wife, may you know the peace of God as you embrace and live the purpose He has for you.

To my granddaughters, Ashlynn, Madi, and Brae, may you find your identity in Jesus and live life large.

To Patti, my assistant and friend, by your willingness to take care of the details, you allow me to pursue the passion of my heart–helping others encounter Jesus. I can never thank you enough.

To Dick and Diane Rush, you will never know how very much you are appreciated. Promise of Hope could not exist without you.

To Bill and Pat Bledsoe, this book would not have happened without your tireless efforts. Thank you for your hours of work.

To the Board of Promise of Hope Ministries, Bill and Pat Bledsoe, Patti and Ken Kimble, Sandy and Phyllis Nutt, and Dick Rush, thank you for your prayers and sacrifices. Sandy, thank you for your help. You have kept us going.

Richard and Beverly Sadowski, you continue to open doors of opportunity to us that allow Promise of Hope to expand. Thank you.

To Bill Amick and Bob McCleskey, thank you for listening to the Lord.

To Wendell and Paula Stratton, your generosity has fueled the growth of Promise of Hope. Thank you for your sacrifice and friendship.

To the Partners of Promise of Hope Ministries, thank you. Neither this ministry nor this book would exist without you. Greg Hatcher, Momma Trish, Rob Kimble, Euell and Peggy Paul, John and Nancy Yates, David and Nancy Baker, and Ken Kimble, thank you.

And a Special Thank You to George and Gail DuBose, and the Liberty Group. Without your involvement, it would have been impossible for us to have experienced all that God has done through Promise of Hope. We especially appreciate Tim Stafford, Victoria Stafford, Jason Ansley, Amy Rice, and all the team at Liberty Group.

To the BGR Team, it is a joy to partner with you.

To Butch and Brenda, thank you for your kindness and friendship. It means more than you will ever know.

To Conrad and Melanie, your friendship is special.

To Jess and Linda Davis, thank you for demonstrating what an enduring friendship really means.

My deepest gratitude goes to my wife, Janice. You have inspired me to trust God and stretch beyond my capacity. Thank you. I love you with all my heart.

My greatest appreciation goes to my Lord Jesus. He has sustained me during the difficult times, and He has blessed me beyond anything I deserve.

Book Dedication

*This book is dedicated to the Remnant;
those who have chosen to stay faithful to
God as our nation accelerates its departure
from Him.*

Foreword

Exposed is a book whose time has come. Chuck McAlister has, through impeccable research, woven together America's history and its current trends and events to provide us with a clear picture of where we have been and where we are going. Seemingly unrelated events and tendencies are shown to have a common denominator that has been overlooked or purposefully ignored by the secular press. We are a nation that is accelerating its departure from God and, therefore, leaving the protection that only He can provide. As Chuck states, "People and nations can die from exposure." America's exposure is increasing in direct proportion to its rapid withdrawal from God. In *Exposed,* Chuck shows us where this departure began in our nation's history, how events like the terrorist attack of September 11, 2001, recent increases in natural disasters, and even our current economic crisis may very well have their roots in our departure from God.

Chuck McAlister is neither rash nor careless. I have known Chuck for many years. His degree in geology uniquely qualifies him to discuss several of the topics in this book. His integrity has insured that the facts of this book have been carefully checked. His love for America, as evidenced by his military service, has required that this book be written with a broken heart. I have seen Chuck's faithful and consistent character in good times and bad. In fact, my relationship with Chuck began after losing my first election and, while pondering my next step, I received a phone call from him offering me the opportunity to work with him until I could determine the direction I would take for my life. Chuck is a friend to those in need. It is no surprise that, in its hour of greatest need, America would experience Chuck reaching out a hand of explanation and assistance to help steer her back on course.

The message of this book is sobering, but true. It is a message that must be shared. If America does not return to God, our exposure will lead to our demise. Join me and many others who are determined to be a part of the Remnant, who have chosen to stay faithful to God as our nation accelerates its departure from Him and maybe, just maybe, we can see the impossible happen. We can see America return to God.

Mike Huckabee

Contents

Introduction

To be "exposed" can carry several meanings. It can describe the condition of being unprotected, at risk. It can also mean the disclosure of something secret or previously unknown. As a book, *Exposed* encompasses both of these meanings. I am convinced that we, as Americans, have forfeited, in recent years, the divine protection that guarded us as a nation. I believe we are a people at risk, exposed to the political elements of this world in ways that are both dangerous and foreboding.

To understand how we arrived at this position of exposure, we must discover the steps we have taken to find ourselves in such a vulnerable position.

While involved in a study of economic depressions and contrasting periods of prosperity in America, I discovered evidence of a consistent pattern. A pattern that, I believe, reveals the reason we find ourselves in such an exposed position. On close examination, I found that this pattern was similar to the divine pattern by which God dealt with the nations of Israel and Judah in the Bible.

By identifying this cycle, we are not just uncovering an interesting pattern or a repetitive sequence of events. It is uplifting and inspiring to realize that our country has a religious heritage that can be compared to the nations of Israel and Judah in Scripture. However, just as the prophets warned Israel and later, Judah, there are dire warnings about the spiritual state of our nation and its subsequent exposure.

As we examine our country's past, you will see along the way the signposts of our departure from God as a nation, the very departure that has left us exposed. As we "expose" the pattern of departure, it is my hope that many people will discover what is happening to our nation and be moved to return to God. People and nations can die from exposure. May we, in America, wake up to the vulnerable position in which we find ourselves and return to the only One who can protect and preserve us.

Chuck McAlister

Chapter One

A Pattern of Return and Renewal

There have been four periods in our past when we have returned to God, as a people, and experienced a nationwide renewal. After careful study, it is evident a consistent pattern of events characterizes each one of these times of renewal. We also find an astounding parallel relationship, demonstrated in Scripture, between our nation, the United States of America, and the nations of Israel and Judah, out of which the heritage of our faith has emerged. I am convinced that this pattern of return and renewal is the means by which God interacts with any nation desiring His protection. To ignore this pattern leaves a nation dangerously exposed.

As we look at this pattern in the history of our nation and others, we see first, a time of financial crisis. During those days of financial uncertainty, people typically turned to God for help. In a panic, many sought to know what God desired for them to do.

Following the financial crisis, there was an interval of brokenness demonstrated by a return to God. As the cycle continued, a great renewal swept across the nation, bringing with it social change and a renewed morality.

After this spiritual renewal, a war occurred. It is as if God prepared us for battle with the renewal. Then a period of prosperity came, followed by another financial crisis. This pattern in our nation's history is the same pattern we see unfold as we study the history of the nation of Israel.

We will look at our past, as a nation, in order to understand how radically America has changed. In subsequent chapters, we will draw parallels with Israel's past to better grasp the pattern of exposure God follows when dealing with a nation.

There have been four periods of renewal in America's past when God moved with great power.

There have been four periods of renewal in America's past when God moved with great power to draw us into an awareness of who He is. The pattern has remained consistent until recent times, when we have seen alarming signs indicating that we have moved away from God and become a nation exposed.

The First Great Awakening

The first great national renewal or awakening in America took place between 1725 and 1760. It began during a time of high taxes, inflation, and impending financial collapse in the colonies.

Benjamin Franklin was so impressed with the impact of this great movement of God that he arranged for an auditorium to be built to accommodate the crowds that regularly came to

15

hear his friend Jonathan Edwards preach. That building became the first structure on the campus of the University of Pennsylvania.[1]

Jonathan Edwards later noted the impact of God's movement in the colonies during this period and stated, "The town seemed to be full of the presence of God, for its men were so full of love and so full of joy."[2] A tremendous return to God broke out and rippled through the colonies with such force that, by the beginning of the American Revolution, 99.8 percent of the colonists claimed to be believers in Jesus Christ.[3] This nation was birthed in the midst of a great spiritual renewal.

This nation was birthed in the midst of a great spiritual renewal.

This sovereign movement of God's Spirit prepared our nation for the Revolutionary War, the next step in our national cycle. Many of those whose hearts were changed in this first spiritual renewal served their country as patriots to win our freedom. Enormous prosperity followed the revolution, but our nation soon put aside the fervor of the First Great Awakening and gave way to materialism. Fueled by the practice of slavery, the pursuit of wealth was rampant in the new nation.

God was merciful, and He continued to bless America. The Lord led us, just a few years after the first great spiritual renewal, into the next Great Awakening.

The Second Great Awakening

The Second Great Awakening lasted from 1787 to 1805. The frontier area of Kentucky and Tennessee had been introduced to a new method of evangelism called circuit preaching. These circuit riding preachers fanned out across our country, most covering a circuit of 200 to 500 miles every two to six weeks.

Frances Asbury, the best known of these preachers, transported everything he owned in two saddlebags and traveled over 270 thousand miles by horseback. Asbury preached over sixteen thousand sermons and saw thousands of people come to Jesus Christ.[4]

A return to God began to sweep eastward from Kentucky and Tennessee as we were launched into this Second Great Awakening. A spiritual renewal gripped our nation as God prepared us for yet another war, the War of 1812. Immediately following this war came a period of expanding trade and prosperity. Then came the third great spiritual renewal in our nation's history.

The Third Great Awakening

It seems that we were not satisfied with the prosperity God had given our nation. A deep greed and the sin of slavery had merged to corrupt our land. By 1857, God was getting our attention by moving our nation into another financial depression, continuing the cycle of returning to Him for spiritual renewal and His protection.

Joseph Lanphier began a noontime prayer meeting in New York City. It grew from one person to ten thousand, moving the entire nation to prayer. Prayer groups formed in places like Louisville, Baltimore, Philadelphia, and New York. As immigrants arrived in this great nation, chaplains stationed at Ellis Island led thousands into a relationship with Jesus Christ. In two years, it was claimed that two million converts were added to the church.[5]

Out of this movement came the Third Great Awakening, lasting from 1857 to 1865. As prayer swept from city to city, many people became convicted that slavery displeased God, and brokenness over our national sin swiftly gained momentum. It was the most intensive awakening our country had ever experienced, as God prepared our nation for the greatest war it had ever faced.

In the midst of this great movement, the Civil War began on April 4, 1861. More Americans were killed during the four-year period of this war than in all other American wars combined. More than 600 thousand men died as our nation was purged of the sin of slavery and greed.[6] Abraham Lincoln stated:

> American slavery is one of those offenses which, in the providence of God... He now wills to remove, and... He gives to both North and South this terrible war as the woe [*judgment*] due to those by whom the offense came.[7]

Through all of this, God continued to preserve our nation because we still had a heart to follow His will and direction. After a difficult period of Reconstruction, the Industrial Revolution fueled one of the greatest periods of prosperity our nation had ever seen and led us into the fourth great movement of God in our history.

> *Through all of this, God continued to preserve our nation because we still had a heart to follow His will and direction.*

19

The Fourth Great Awakening

The Fourth Great Awakening began in 1904 and lasted until 1910. Another major depression had struck in 1893. Credit was excessive. In America, six hundred banks and fifteen thousand companies failed within a period of a few months. In distress, people were moved to seek God through prayer.

Spiritual renewal began to break out in Wales, England between 1900 and 1904. It was so intense that jails sat empty and judges had no cases to try.[8] Churches were filled for days on end as people came to pray. Sporting events could not be conducted. People were too busy seeking God.[9] Revival spread across the Atlantic to America, and from 1904 to 1910 a movement of the Spirit of God swept our country. The population of New England was 340 thousand during this time. It is estimated that the renewal brought 50 thousand people to salvation.[10]

The war that this awakening prepared us for was World War I. Then came the Roaring '20s and an explosion of economic prosperity. But, for America, the pattern began to break down at this point.

The Pattern Broken

Following the dramatic economic growth of the 1920s, came the most devastating financial collapse our nation had ever experienced. The Great Depression began in 1929 followed by World War II, but there was no spiritual renewal following the Great Depression. There was no brokenness, and no massive return to God occurred, neither was there a great spiritual renewal on a scale such as in the Great Awakenings of the past.

World War II was followed by Korea, Vietnam, Desert Storm, Kosovo, and now the War on Terror, the longest war in the history of America. But still there has been no evidence of a great spiritual renewal among the people of our nation.

These wars were not of the same magnitude as World Wars I and II, but according to the pattern of the protection of God in the past, there should have been a spiritual renewal to prepare us for each of these conflicts. There was not!

Unless a nation returns to God in brokenness over its departure, that nation will not experience the blessing of a spiritual renewal. But, if people within that nation return to God and seek His presence and favor, God will insure that the people of that nation not only experience spiritual renewal, but His protection as well. He will not leave them exposed.

> *What happened to break the pattern in America?*

What happened to break the pattern in America? Some parts of the pattern have continued. We have had severe financial declines, wars, and periods of economic boom, but no more spiritual renewals. Why?

Let's go back to where we got off track. We had a spiritual renewal to prepare us for World War I. It began in Europe and spread to America, and helped both Europe and America prepare for that war.

However, there was another battle during that same period. It started in the early 1920s as a struggle for the heart of America. It wasn't fought with bullets and artillery, but it was, nonetheless, a major war, and it continues to this day.

This battle was waged with the sophisticated and sometimes devious weapons of ideas. The enemy took on the forms of Karl Marx, Charles Darwin, Sigmund Freud, and Friedrich Nietzsche. They were infusing new ways of thinking into the Western World in great contrast to the concepts, ideas, and beliefs traditionally held by the people of our nation. Their ideas fought for the hearts of Americans and still continue to mislead many to this day.

Sigmund Freud introduced the idea that the world revolved around sexual dysfunction, and we became a nation preoccupied with sex.

Karl Marx advocated social revolution, the abolition of personal property, and the sacrifice of individual rights for the benefit of the state. As a consequence, much of our nation became a people who had lost their personal ambition.

Charles Darwin challenged the Biblical account of our origin by teaching that we were not created, but that we evolved from animals. The logic followed that we may as well live like animals with all the violence that this entails. The central theme of our existence became, like that of animals, self-preservation.

Friedrich Nietzsche added the crowning touch to this departure from God. In a total rejection of the existence of God, he announced that, "God is dead."[11] America, emerging from a rich heritage of spiritual renewal and God's protection, became a nation preoccupied with sex, devoid of personal ambition, enamored with self-preservation, and without meaning and purpose in life. We became unfulfilled, empty, and without hope because we stopped listening to God and began listening to men.

God moved to get our attention in 1929 through the Great Depression. Over 25 percent of our nation's work force was unemployed. Suicide became the leading cause of death in America.[12] Still, there was no national return to God or spiritual renewal.

Throughout the 1930s, the Great Depression continued. The natural disaster of the Dust Bowl, a merciless drought, struck in the Midwest severely crippling our farmers and choking the economy of our entire country. Even then, there was no return to God.

Then we entered the decade of the 1940s, and on December 7, 1941, Japan attacked Pearl Harbor. Our country was suddenly hurled into the cruel depths of World War II. Our role changed from being the supplier of weapons and munitions for the free world, to being completely committed by sending our young men into the horrors of war. The 1940s proved to be a bloody decade, marred by World War II, the Holocaust, atomic bombs, and the launching of the Cold War.

> *Yet, there was no brokenness and no widespread turning to God for protection.*

In the face of such a gruesome situation, and realizing the severity of the threat to the entire free world, wouldn't it be expected that our nation would experience a turning to God? Yet, there was no brokenness and no widespread turning to God for protection.

During the decade of the 1950s, churches began to flourish, or so it seemed. At first, it appeared that a post-war spiritual renewal was about to begin outside the traditional pattern of prosperity, financial crisis, return to God, spiritual renewal, and then war.

It soon became evident, however, that this renewal was superficial. Churches emerged that were more interested in institutional survival than in changing lives. As a nation, we went through the motions of being religious without promoting a growing relationship with God through Jesus Christ. We embraced our values and convinced ourselves that we did not need to return to God.

Something had happened to the heart and mind of America. The ideas birthed in the 1920s by men like Freud, Darwin, Marx, and Nietzsche took root in our educational and judicial systems and were beginning to take hold in the minds of many Americans.

Numerous churches sought to synthesize these ideas with Christianity. Many of the men who filled the pulpits of our churches didn't believe in the basic tenets of the Christian faith. They rejected the truth of Scripture for a watered down gospel of relativism. The 1950s were dominated by Elvis, the birth of television, the beginning of Rock and Roll, economic growth, the emergence of the teen culture, and the Cold War which spawned yet another armed conflict, the Korean War. Our preoccupation, as a nation, became living The American Dream.

The first issue of *Playboy* was published in the 1950s, indicating how readily the nation had embraced Freud's ideas, demonstrating our growing preoccupation with sex, and laying the groundwork for the sexual revolution to come.

Our ministers did not call the people of our nation to return to God, and so there was no brokenness and no spiritual renewal. Our judicial and educational systems were already beginning to accept many anti-Christian concepts spawned by the ideas of the 1920s.

The 1960s and 1970s brought a wave of rebellion. A rage was brewing that produced the hippie generation and gave birth to a new counter culture. The 1960s were tumultuous as Americans became disillusioned and questioned all authority. It was a time of violence, from Vietnam to the civil rights movement. The media demonstrated the confusion being felt by the country, with music emerging as the primary means of expression. Every foundational belief was called into question. The post-World War II baby boom had created 70 million teenagers, and they dominated the culture.

The Jesus movement of the 1960s sparked pockets of spiritual renewal, but it was never embraced by mainstream America and subsequently declined as the young people who gave rise to it were institutionalized by the church in the 1970s. The 1960s ended with America confused and divided, and still there was no return to God.

The decade of the 1970s began with a sense of frustration because of the continuing war in Vietnam, and ended with a sense of despair characterized by the hostage crisis in Iran, which seemed to give further evidence of a national decline. We witnessed the accelerated unraveling of the moral fiber of our nation as we experienced the growing acceptance of the sexual revolution by the general population, the first ever resignation of a sitting president, and the Supreme Court decision *Roe v. Wade*, which legitimized the killing of the unborn. We were seeing the continued influence of the ideas of the 1920s as they became the shapers of our nation. By the end of the 1970s, our nation had still experienced no return to God and no spiritual renewal. Our morals, as a people, were slipping, and we were slipping further away from God.

The 1980s began with double digit inflation. Binge buying and credit cards became the way of life. This was the "me" decade of hostile takeovers, mega-mergers, and leveraged buyouts. It was the time for baby boomers to splurge on everything from camcorders to minivans. We were determined to live The American Dream, even if we had to do it on credit. For the first time we defined ourselves by the stuff with which we surrounded ourselves rather than the content of our hearts.

The 1980s invited us into the Reagan Revolution and a return to conservative ideas, but President Ronald Reagan himself rarely attended church. Ideas with no spiritual foundation cannot bring about spiritual renewal. The 1980s realized no return to God. They did, however, end with a ray of hope. The collapse of the Berlin Wall seemed to remove the sting of the 1986 Challenger disaster. The ray of hope was short lived, however.

The decade of the 1990s emerged as a decade of discovery and violence. The Hubble Telescope was launched into space, cloning was introduced, and in 1992, the internet began and was boasting 100 million participants on the web by the end of the decade. While the economy was booming with record low unemployment and the stock market at an all-time high, it was something other than a good economy that defined the 1990s. Internationally, America found itself acting as policeman of the world, facing wars and violent situations in the Persian Gulf, Somalia, Haiti, Bosnia, and Yugoslavia. Domestically, we had become a nation whose declining morals had given rise to increased violence. In 1993, we experienced our first terrorist attack with the explosion of a bomb in the garage of the World Trade Center in New York City. The same year gave us the deadly raid on the Branch Davidian Compound in Waco, Texas. In 1995, one of our own citizens, Timothy McVeigh, bombed the federal building in Oklahoma City killing 168, including nineteen children under the age of six and injuring more than 680 people.[13] From February 1996 to April 1999, there were at least fourteen incidents of school shootings in America. The most deadly was at Columbine High School in Littleton, Colorado where fifteen were killed and twenty-three were wounded.[14]

Through the 1990s, we allowed the ideas espoused by Freud, Marx, Darwin, and Nietzsche to become engrained in our national psyche. We watched our morals continue to deteriorate until our children were shooting each other. While the 1990s were characterized by ever increasing levels of violence, it must be remembered that the root cause of this violence was found in the ideas we were teaching our children. The most damaging of those ideas grows out of Frederick Nietzsche's assertion that "God is dead." Once a nation begins to live as if there is no God, then it is a small step to believe that there is no such thing as truth. Everything becomes relative to the needs or whims of the individual. All moral moorings are lost. Nietzsche, himself, stated: "There are no facts, only interpretations."[15] The view that there is no such thing as truth began to gain widespread acceptance in our nation in the 1990s. The result was no foundation on which to base our morals. With the rejection of truth as an absolute, moral relativism evolved into moral permissiveness.

It should not be surprising that our nation would be guilty of the extreme tolerance of accepting the indiscretions of a morally bankrupt president during the decade of the 1990s, given how far we had declined by this time. We were so absent of indignation that we yawned in the face of his immorality, and we still refused to return to God. So it was that, even to the very end of the decade of the 1990s, we still had no return to God and no spiritual renewal. The pattern of return and renewal seemed irrevocably broken.

The dawn of the new millennium found America conflicted. The decade began with hanging chads and a highly contested presidential election that sounded more like a third world country exchange of power than the peaceful exchange of power based on the vote of the people, to which our republic had been accustomed. The defining moment for the first decade of 2000 occurred on September 11, 2001 with the attack on the Twin Towers in New York and the Pentagon, as well as the crash of Flight 93 in a field in Pennsylvania. These were a series of coordinated suicide attacks by al-Qaeda, killing 2,995 people.[16] The United States subsequently launched the war on terror, which has become the longest running war in the history of our nation.

The first decade of 2000, while defined by the attacks of 9-11, was the decade of superlatives: The longest lasting war, the largest Ponzi scheme in the history of man thanks to Berni Madoff, the worst natural disaster in our nation's history—Hurricane Katrina, an economy on the brink of total destruction, and a president who increased the national debt more than any other president in U.S. history while espousing conservative ideals.

As *Time Magazine* stated:

> Bookended by 9-11 at the start and financial wipeout at the end, the first ten years of this century will very likely go down as the most dispiriting and disillusioning decade Americans have lived through....[17]

The relativism and violence of the 1990s gave way to the greed and selfishness of the

31

2000s, and a mountain of financial problems from record numbers of bank closures and corporate bankruptcies to a stock market that was down 26 percent as the decade came to a close. *Time Magazine* continued:

> ...so here's the big question: Why? Why did so much bad stuff happen in this decade?[18] ... In large part, we have ourselves to blame. If you look at the underlying causes of some of the most troubling developments of the decade, you can see some striking common denominators....[19]

The common denominators, which this article identify as the reasons this decade has been so difficult, in my opinion, are the culmination of the last ninety years of our refusal to return to God. They are:

1. Neglect[20] When we choose to live as if God doesn't exist, we not only lose our sense of purpose and meaning in life, but we also lose our awareness of reality. We look only inward. As a result of this narcissistic approach to life, we refused to notice the warning signs that Islamic terrorism was approaching our shores. Nietzsche's idea regarding God and truth has born its fruit in our nation.

2. Greed[21] Since we have embraced Darwin's idea of our origin as animals, then it follows that the focus of our existence, like that of animals, becomes self-preservation. We are motivated to gather and selfishly keep all we can. The housing bubble of cheap money and excessive borrowing, which nearly collapsed the economy of our nation, was driven by one thing: greed–men living like animals.

3. Self-Interest[22] Freud added yet another dimension to this emerging selfishness by emphasizing the sexual self-interest that he claimed dominates our relationships. Relationships are not only damaged, but destroyed, when we only focus on getting our own needs met. Isn't that exactly what happened to cause the collapse of the auto industry as management and labor embraced in one bad contract after another, assisted by the tawdry politicians who climbed into bed with them? Relationships cannot be successfully maintained when self-interest dominates.

4. Deferral of Responsibility[23] Karl Marx taught us that we need to defer all responsibility to the state and give up your rights, your property, and your ambition. Our infrastructure needs attention: the power grid needs to be upgraded and our bridges are collapsing. Embracing Marx's idea, we just hoped that someone else would handle the problem. New Orleans flooded in 2005 because those who should have fixed the levees didn't.

The first decade of the 2000s ended with no brokenness, no return to God, and no spiritual renewal. The pattern of return and renewal in our nation has been shattered.

Has God been silent all this time, ignoring our failure to return to Him as we have systematically rejected His truth? Or has He withdrawn from us and become inactive in the direction America is moving?

No! God has given us every opportunity to turn around, even though we have persisted in being a rebellious people. We have not experienced a great return to God and subsequent spiritual renewal for the last ninety years. When there is no sorrow for sin, there can be no return to God.

When there is no sorrow for sin, there can be no return to God.

Neither the hardships of the 1930s nor the bloodshed of the 1940s caused us to come back to the God who had so obviously been the driving force behind our start as a nation. Instead, we moved into the superficiality of the 1950s only to be followed by the rebellion of the 1960s and the despair of the

1970s. Rather than respond to this despair by returning to God, we further solidified our departure from God and the subsequent unraveling of our moral fiber by launching a holocaust against the unborn children of our nation. These actions gave rise to the selfishness of the 1980s, and ultimately, the violence of the 1990s. Still, there was no return to God, and America lost its soul and its hope. The citizens of our nation became focused on themselves, giving rise to the extreme greed of the first decade of 2000, which nearly destroyed our economy and the system of free enterprise which works so well in moral nations.

As the first decade of the new millennium drew to a close, we elected a new president who promised change. It was this same president, as a candidate, who stated in an unguarded moment at a fund raiser:

> You go into these small towns in Pennsylvania, and like a lot of small towns in the Midwest, the jobs have been gone now for twenty-five years, and nothing's replaced them. And it's not surprising then, they get bitter, they cling to guns, or religion, or antipathy to people who aren't like them….to explain their frustrations.[24]

35

God has been relegated to the status of dealing with whatever frustrations are present until the real answer to all our problems can be implemented. The greed of the first decade of 2000 demonstrates that the ideas spawned in the 1920s now completely dominate our culture.

The pattern has been completely broken, and there is no evidence that a return to God and corresponding spiritual renewal is anywhere on the horizon for America. What does this mean for the future of America? It means that we are a nation exposed, which carries ominous forebodings for our future. The following chapters will reveal where we are heading as a nation and what, I believe, God is doing about it.

Chapter Two

The First Step of Exposure: God Reveals the Nation's Prosperity

There are four steps that God takes when a nation pulls away from Him, breaking the pattern of return and renewal.

As a nation begins to pull away from God and His protection, God does not punish or wreak havoc on that nation. Instead, He reminds the nation how involved He has been in their formation and cultivation as a people.

His first act is to bless the people of that nation, showing them His grace and mercy. God gives the nation an opportunity to return to Him and avoid the consequences of removing itself from His protection, revealing to it just how much He has blessed it. Isaiah describes God's process of first revealing the benefits He has shown the nation that has fallen away from Him.

Isaiah 5

1. "I will sing for the one I love
a song about his vineyard:
My loved one had a vineyard
on a fertile hillside.
2. He dug it up and cleared it of
stones, and planted it with the
choicest vines.
He built a watchtower in it
and cut out a winepress as well;
Then he looked for a crop of
good grapes, but it yielded only
bad fruit."

This is a parable in the form of a song. It is a country song, or a ballad, about a man who constructed a vineyard. He put the very best of everything into it. But when it came time for it to bear fruit, it only produced "bad fruit." The vineyard was a tremendous disappointment to him.

This parable has a very powerful message for us. The vineyard represents the nation of Israel, but it can apply to any nation that has been blessed by God, only to rebel against Him later. "The vineyard of the Lord Almighty is the house of Israel..." (Isaiah 5:7a). The same steps God followed in exposing Israel are unfolding in His exposure of America.

The parable tells us that the vineyard was "on a fertile hillside." This informs us that Palestine was a fertile place. The people of Israel were bountifully blessed, living in a land of milk and honey. It was good, fruitful ground. However, it produced a bad crop of grapes.

This is especially applicable to America. We are known as the breadbasket of the world. We grow enough food to feed a large part of the world, single-handedly. God has blessed us. We are a very "fertile hillside."

Notice also, in Isaiah 5:2 that, "He dug it up." This means that he dug a moat around the vineyard, planting a hedge around it for protection from animals and thieves, and cultivated the soil for optimum production. These actions distinguished his vineyard from the other vineyards. They made his vineyard different. It was separated from the other vineyards of the area by the special attention it was given.

God separates those He loves and intends to use. When God plans to use a nation, He separates that nation from the world to mark it as distinct and different, and He gives it a divine purpose to fulfill. God used the law as a hedge to separate Israel from other nations.

> *God separates those He loves and intends to use.*

God used our religious heritage to separate America from other nations. North America, especially the United States, and South America were settled at the same time. North America was settled so that those who were seeking God could express their religious beliefs. South America was settled, not for God, but for gold and greed.

Look at the difference! The United States of America is exceptionally blessed and extremely prosperous. With the blessing of God's hand on us, we have sent His Truth to the far corners of the world, while much of South America is made up of third world countries plagued by poverty and disease.

Isaiah 5:2 tells us the vineyard owner, "dug it up and cleared it of stones." In the original language, this verse indicated a personal and tender involvement with the vineyard by the owner. He dug it up by hand. In other words, with love and care, he cultivated his vineyard with his own hands.

God's hand has been on the United States of America just as His hand was on the nation of Israel. The same loving care the owner of the vineyard bestowed upon His vineyard, Israel, He has bestowed upon America. God has truly blessed America.

The Scripture also indicates that the owner of the vineyard cleared out the stones from the vineyard. God wanted all hindrances removed.

God told Israel to remove the Canaanites from their land, but Israel didn't listen. It left the stumbling blocks inside its nation. This act of disobedience ultimately led to the exposure of their nation.

Like Israel, our nation's greatest enemies are not those outside our country, but those within our country. The spreading of anti-Christian ideas, rooted in those ideas introduced in the 1920s, are the stumbling blocks to our spiritual heritage. God has sought to remove these stumbling blocks from our midst just as He sought to do for Israel.

For the ideas of the 1920s that caused us to wander away from Him, God allowed the hardships of the 1930s and the Great Depression, but there was no return to Him by our nation. God has done all He can to preserve us and protect us from the stumbling blocks that would lead to our destruction, but we seem bent on suffering the consequences of exposure they cause.

It seems that we have become hardened and have failed to respond to God's merciful interventions. Like Israel, we have failed to oust ideas from our nation that continue to corrupt us.

Israel was God's choice vine, in Isaiah's day, to be a light to the world. I believe America was God's choice vine in the contemporary world. We were called out, a melting pot of nations and peoples, to be a spiritual light in the modern world.

As the world's economic, political, and military leader, our influence was never greater. In 1967, Richard Wurmbrand, a great Romanian pastor who was imprisoned fourteen years for his faith, wrote, "Every freedom-loving man has two fatherlands, his own and America."[25] America is the hope of every enslaved man because America means freedom in the world.

However, we are using our influence to export our materialistic culture rather than the truth about God and His Son, Jesus. God is allowing us to be exposed for our rebellion, and He will continue this exposure until we return to Him and begin to fulfill our purpose to be a light to the nations for Christ.

We find that, "He built a watchtower in it..." (v. 2) to watch over the vineyard. This vineyard was set on a hill (v. 1). The original language literally means a mountain peak. From a tower on a mountain peak, a vast panorama of the surrounding land can be surveyed.

This vineyard occupies a prominent position, as Israel was the most prominent nation in the world during the time of Isaiah. Israel had just defeated Egypt, the most feared nation in the world, and had earned its place of importance.

America also enjoys a place of prominence among the nations in today's world. As President Reagan once described us, we are "a city set on a hill," enjoying a panoramic view of the rest of the world. We have been watching over world affairs ever since we defeated Great Britain in the American Revolutionary War. The collapse of the Soviet Union thrust us into an even greater prominence as we became the dominant world power.

From its beginning, America has been a nation of destiny and vision. Discovered and settled by men and women who were driven by God-given visions, the history of America is the story of God's preparation of a people to touch the world with the good news of Jesus Christ.

Our position of prominence has been arranged by God to help us fulfill the purpose for which God has called us. God has been making us a tower of His grace.

> *God has been making us a tower of His grace.*

When Christopher Columbus resolved to find a route to the West Indies, he wrote the following entries in his diary:

43

> It was the Lord who put into my mind... to sail to the Indies.... There is no question that the inspiration was from the Holy Spirit.... No one should be afraid to take on any task in the name of our Savior if the intention is purely for His holy service....[26]

On October 12, 1492, he landed on the first island of the New World and named it San Salvador, which means "Our Savior." Columbus waded ashore, and He then prayed:

> "O Lord, Almighty and everlasting God... praised be Thy Majesty... that Thy holy Name may be proclaimed in this second part of the earth."[27]

Columbus proclaimed the destiny of every piece of ground he discovered by planting a large wooden cross on its shore. He prayed that this land would not belong to any country, but to God Almighty Himself.

From its very discovery, it is obvious that God intended for America to be a tower set on a hill to shine the light of the gospel into the world. America has been chosen and called to a great purpose.

God's provision to help Israel remain faithful to its God-given purpose is illustrated in

44

Isaiah 5:2, "...and [I] cut out a winepress." The winepress was used to crush grapes to extract the juice. It was a place of brokenness. God gave Israel the ceremonial sacrificial system to keep them broken before Him and to remind them of the coming Messiah.

America has also been given a winepress, the winepress of God's Word, to keep us broken and humble before Him. There is practically a church on every street corner in our nation and more Bibles than we can count. God's Word should be used by us as the tool of judgment in our lives. Yet, we have forsaken God's Word by refusing to apply it to our lives. We have taken God's Word for granted.

We have the Word of God available to us as no other people on earth have ever had. It is estimated that 92 percent of American households own a Bible, and most homes have at least three copies.[28] As pollster George Barna commented, "Americans revere the Bible, but they don't read the Bible."[29]

Since we refuse to allow ourselves to be exposed to the winepress of God's Word, God's exposure of us will continue, step by step, until we return to Him or face the conclusion of the exposure.

Notice, in the latter part of verse 2 it says, "...then he looked for a crop of good grapes, but it yielded only bad fruit." Literally translated, *bad fruit* reads *sour berries*.

This scripture was referring to the nation of Israel producing bad fruit. Because we have refused to let God's Word correct us and have not heeded God's warning, America has also been producing bad fruit.

Isaiah 5

> 3. *"Now you dwellers in Jerusalem and men of Judah, judge between me and my vineyard.*
> *4. What more could have been done for my vineyard than I have done for it?*
> *When I looked for good grapes, why did it yield only bad?"*

Can you sense that God is heartbroken? He says that He could not have given any more blessings to these people than He has given them, and in return, they have borne bad fruit.

> *Can you sense that God is heartbroken?*

As a nation, we too, are bearing bad fruit. Instead of exporting the gospel, we are exporting a culture that seeks to ignore God. Osama Bin Laden and his followers said, in regard to the events surrounding September 11, 2001, that Americans have become an evil and decadent people. Terrorist leaders want no part of our culture or our commodities.

It grieved my heart to hear this as it was broadcast on a national news program. We should be exporting the truth to other nations in order to set their people free. But instead, we are exporting a culture whose emphasis is materialism and whose focus is self, not God. I can almost hear God saying to America, "What more could I have done to bless this people?"

The first step of exposure is for God to remind the nation bent on leaving Him of the blessings He has given them. I am convinced that God has long since taken this first step of exposure regarding America. By blessing us in spite of our rebellion, He has revealed to us the source of our prosperity, but we have taken our prosperity for granted and have failed to acknowledge that God is its source. What happens when the first step of exposure doesn't bring about a return to God? God takes the next step of exposure.

Chapter Three

The Second Step of Exposure: God Removes the Nation's Protection

The first step God takes in His exposure of a nation is to reveal to the nation its prosperity. If that doesn't bring about a national movement to return to Him, He then proceeds to the second step. God removes His protection from that nation.

God shows what this second step of exposure looks like as He describes His interaction with Israel:

Isaiah 5

5. "Now I will tell you what I am going to do to my vineyard: I will take away its hedge, and it will be destroyed; I will break down its wall, and it will be trampled.
6. I will make it a wasteland, neither pruned nor cultivated, and briers

*and thorns will grow there. I will
command the clouds not to rain on
it."*
*7(a). The vineyard of the Lord Al-
mighty is the house of Israel, and the
men of Judah are the garden of His
delight.*

God declares that He will remove the
hedge of His protection from Israel, His vineyard, because they wandered away from Him.
The nation had deserted the purpose that God
called it to fulfill. Notice, however, that even as
God removes the hedge of protection from the
nation that has pulled away from Him, He does
so professing His love for His people. He tells
the people of the Southern Kingdom of Judah,
who are watching the self-destruction of the
Northern Kingdom, that they are His "delight."
Nevertheless, He must take the nation He loves
into the second step of exposure.

What causes God to remove His protection from a nation (or an individual) that He has
begun to expose? In verse 7 we can find the answer.

Isaiah 5

7(b). And He looked for justice, but saw bloodshed; for righteousness, but heard cries of distress.

God looked for good fruit in the nation that He expected to be living out His purpose. He looked for justice, but instead, God found bloodshed and cries of distress in a violent nation.

In short, when God shows a nation the benefits it enjoys as a result of its relationship with Him, the nation finds itself at a crossroad. It can respond by returning to God with a broken heart over its rebellion, or it can choose to career headlong down the path it has chosen for itself—a path of continuing distance between itself and God.

I am convinced that God took America into the first step of exposure in the post-World War II economic boom of the 1950s. He was demonstrating to America that we were His "delight." We found ourselves at a crucial crossroad. We could respond to the many benefits we enjoyed as a result of our relationship with God by returning to Him and experiencing the spiritual renewal that would put us back on track with His pattern of protection. Or we could continue to embrace the ideas spawned in our culture in the 1920s, and thus, force God to move us into the second step of exposure.

What was America's choice? We responded to God's expression of love for us and the benefits He had given us, as a people, with the rebellion of the 1960s. We told God that we did not want to return to Him, and with a broken heart, God took us as a nation into the second step of exposure.

What is the evidence that a nation has obstinately refused to return to God and has been moved into this second step of exposure? It is "bloodshed" or violence coupled with "cries of distress." The people of that nation become a violent people, and the "cries of distress" fill the nation. Have we seen this happen since the 1960s in America?

The US Department of Justice predicted that, in 1996, eighty-three percent of all Americans were likely to be victims of violent crime at least once in their lifetime.[30] One violent crime occurred every seventeen seconds, one murder every twenty-three minutes, one forcible rape every five minutes, one robbery every fifty-one seconds, one aggravated assault every twenty-eight seconds, one burglary every twelve seconds, one larceny theft every four seconds, and one child died of gunshot wounds every two hours.[31]

Did you know that the typical American child, in 1996, was fifteen times more likely to be killed by gunfire than a child born in strife-torn Northern Ireland?[32] In 1996, according to the Department of Justice, 538 American children were murdered by their own parents, and 308 parents were murdered by their own children.[33]

The homicide rate overall in America nearly doubled from the 1960s to the late 1970s. It declined in the 1980s, only to rise again sharply in the 1990s.[34] The violent crime rate then fell sharply, declining by 41 percent from 1999 to 2008.[35] According to these statistics, violent crime within our nation rose dramatically in the 1960s and 1970s, ebbed downward, and then rose drastically in the 1990s only to return to the pre-1960s level for the first decade of 2000.

As a nation, we were twice given the opportunity to return to God, once in the 1960s and 1970s then again in the 1990s. The violence ebbed in our nation, but we refused to see what it indicated about us, and we refused to return to God.

Drifting away from the truth of God, and subsequently embracing and enhancing the radical ideas born in the 1920s, with no indication of a return to God, left our nation producing bad fruit. When we removed prayer and Bible study from our schools, we sent America's young people a clear message that God and the Bible were irrelevant to their lives.

We reaped a harvest of violence and bloodshed in our nation because of our abandonment of God's truth. God had removed His hedge of protection from our nation, and we refused to notice it.

In the 1960s, there were 160 violent crimes per 100 thousand Americans. By 1996, violent crime had skyrocketed to 634 per 100 thousand Americans—a 396 percent increase. Violent crime by juveniles had soared by 240 percent from 1970 to the mid-1990s. Young people under the age of twenty-one committed almost one-half of all violent crimes in America during the 1990s. Following the tragedy at Columbine High School, Paul Harvey said it well: "No generation in American history has ever been terrified by its offspring, until now."[36]

> *God has removed His hedge of protection from our nation.*

Why didn't we notice the warning sign of "bloodshed" and the "cries of distress"? Why didn't we return to God? Because we had become a selfish and greedy people.

God looked for justice in America, but He saw "bloodshed." He looked for righteousness, but heard "cries of distress" from the victims of violence. He hears the unborn as they cry in distress because of the violence done against them.

When He sees violence to this degree in a nation that is experiencing His prosperity while continuing on with its rebellion, God knows that nation does not intend to return to Him. God then moves that nation into the second step of exposure in which He removes their hedge of protection and allows that nation to proceed without the benefit of His protection or direction.

> *God knows that nation does not intend to return to Him.*

When God removes His protection, six things happen to indicate that the nation or individual is exposed. These actions do not cause the hedge of God's protection to be removed from the nation in rebellion. They are signs that the exposure is progressing and that the hedge of God's protection has already been removed from that nation.

These six indicators are mentioned in Isaiah 5:8-23 and are each marked as a "woe" related specifically to the removal of God's protection. It is important to note that these indicators intensify as the nation being exposed persists in its rebellion by refusing to return to God.

Indicator One: Greed

Isaiah 5

8. Woe to you who add house to house and join field to field till no space is left and you live alone in the land.
9. The LORD Almighty has declared in my hearing: "Surely the great houses will become desolate, the fine mansions left without occupants.
10. A ten-acre vineyard will produce only a bath of wine, a homer of seed only an ephah of grain."

Israel had neglected God's guidelines for the land. They violated the Sabbath rest for the land when they abandoned the Year of Jubilee. During this time the land was to revert back to the original owner, and the land was to rest from cultivation so that it could be rejuvenated.

They craved more and more, adding house to house and field to field so that, according to Isaiah 5:10, a ten-acre vineyard yielded less than ten gallons of juice, and a field of planted seed yielded a harvest of less than a bushel. They ignored God's guidelines on how to handle their possessions until their greed eventually resulted in famine and desolation.

The picture God presents of a nation whose people are exposed is dramatic. The people of the exposed nation show an unrestrained greed demonstrated by the building of more and bigger houses, adding "house to house", coupled with real estate speculation as they join "field to field." To satisfy this inordinate greed, resources are diverted from those areas that could bolster the nation's productivity to benefit its people. The end result of this unbridled greed is a corresponding decline in the productivity of the nation.

In short, once a nation moves into the second step of exposure, it starts a downward economic spiral fueled by the greed of the people to build more and bigger houses. This downward spiral progressively deepens as long as the nation refuses to return to God. He states that the exposed nation will see "...the great houses ...become desolate, the fine mansions left without occupants" (Isaiah 5:9).

The description we are given of the deepening economic crisis of a nation refusing to return to God reads like an analysis of the economic meltdown of the first decade of the new millennium in America. The *Washington Post* characterized the U.S. housing bubble meltdown which led us to the brink of financial collapse by stating:

The impact of the real estate crash has been broad... and as the housing meltdown cascaded through credit markets, the banking system was buffered, rocking the whole financial system.... Capital was funneled to build mini-mansions in Sun Belt suburbs, many of which now sit empty, rather than toward industrial machines or other business investments that might generate economic output and jobs for years to come.... Total household debt rose 117% from 1999 to its peak in 2008... as Americans borrowed to buy ever more expensive homes....[37]

This greed identifies our nation as a nation exposed. Its refusal to return to God is creating an ever deepening economic crisis for America. The first decade of 2000 was the worst for the U.S. economy in modern times. Since December 1999, there has been zero net job creation. No previous decade since the 1940s had job growth less than 20 percent.[38] Economic output rose at its slowest rate of any decade since the 1930s. In other words, our productivity has declined. The first decade of the century was the first decade of falling median incomes since figures were first compiled in the 1960s. The net worth of American house-holds, which posted sharp increases in every previous decade, showed declines for the first time since this data was collected in the 1950s. For most of the past seventy years, the U.S. economy has grown at a steady pace. That changed dramatically with the first decade of 2000.[39]

Our greed, as a people, shows no sign of slowing down. Credit cards continue to be our predominant means of exchange, as our desire for instant gratification envelopes every part of our lives. In 2009, the average American consumer had a total of thirteen credit obligations, nine of which were likely to be credit cards, and four were likely to be installment loans. The average consumer's oldest obligation was fourteen years, indicating that he or she has been managing debt for some time.[40] The average credit card debt per household, with credit card debt, was $15,788.[41] The U.S. credit card outstanding debt was $772.19 billion at the beginning of 2010.[42]

It is not just the people of America who are swimming in debt. America has become a debtor nation. The co-chairs of President Obama's Debt and Deficit Commission, Alan Simpson, former Republican Senator of Wyoming, and Erskine Bowles, White House Chief of Staff under former President Bill Clinton, were assigned the overwhelming task of attempting to address the economic collapse of the first decade of the new century.

"The commission leaders said that, at present, available federal revenues are fully consumed by just three programs: Social Security, Medicare, and Medicaid. 'The rest of the federal government, including fighting two wars, homeland security, education, art, culture, …the whole rest of the discretionary budget is being financed by China and other countries,' Simpson said."[43]

We have become a debtor nation, living exposed to the whims of those to whom we are obligated. Our greed will continue to unravel the fiscal and moral fiber of our nation until we return to God.

> *We have become a debtor nation.*

Another sign of this greed is the explosion of legalized gambling. Shockingly, state and local governments who seek the resulting revenue, now sanction this form of sophisticated robbery.

One of the most abhorrent results of our greed is seen in how we treat the unborn children of our nation. Make no mistake; greed is the driving force behind abortion. The prospective mother says to herself, "I can't afford this baby." We, as a nation, would rather murder our babies than lower our lifestyle or face the inconvenience of having a child that would cause us to change how we live. In our greed, we destroy those we are supposed to love—our children! Many children often grow up neglected and ignored, because Mom and Dad are busy working so that they can afford to live the American Dream.

Since the Scripture tells us that judgment must begin at the House of God, the evidences of the exposure of our nation must surely be seen in the contemporary Church. Consider the "name it and claim it" theology that has invaded congregations all across America. The churches that have been infiltrated with this belief claim that it is our God-given right to be wealthy. In doing so, they are embracing greed as their creed.

Jim Bakker of *PTL* fame knows the danger of greed's influence on the church. His ministry collapsed, and he was imprisoned as the result of his own unbridled greed. Broken and searching for God, Jim embarked on a soul-searching study of the New Testament and radically changed his viewpoint. In his book, *I Was Wrong*, he confesses,

> I even got to the point to where I was teaching people in *PTL*, Don't pray, 'God, Your will be done,' when praying for health or wealth. You al-

ready know it is God's will for you to have those things. Instead of praying 'God's will be done,' when you want a new car, just claim it! Pray specifically, and be sure to specify what options, and what color you want, too." Jim Bakker, with his eyes opened, continued, "Such arrogance. Such foolishness. Such sin.[44]

This philosophy has captured the hearts of many churches in America today. Unfortunately, Jim Bakker is an exception. He woke up. But it took the failure of his ministry, the harsh hand of justice, and the painful experience of prison to prepare his heart to seek the truth.

> *Many churches continue to be trapped in this materialistic mentality.*

Many churches continue to be trapped in this materialistic mentality. We are a people craving for possessions. The example of Jim Bakker is verification that this type of materialism is radically influencing our churches.

It has impacted every facet of American life, from our sense of morality to our relationships, from the choices we make about our daily activities to the candidates we support, from our churches to our children. Greed is so widespread that it touches practically every area of our lives. It is one of the surest signs that we are a nation exposed. In recent years, our greed has taken yet another form as we are driven to get the latest and best technological gadget from computers to cell phones to whatever has just been released. We just can't live without it. We are a nation exposed, and we obstinately refuse to return to God.

Jesus asked, "For what profit is it to a man if he gains the whole world, and is himself destroyed or lost?"[45] He told a parable to illustrate that greed is one of the surest indicators of exposure not only in nations, but individuals as well. The parable tells us of a man who was totally dominated by his greed. He was already living exposed, but he refused to see it. The end of his earthly life was eminent. That night, God confronted the man.

Luke 12

16. And he told them this parable: "The ground of a certain rich man produced a good crop.
17. He thought to himself, 'What shall I do, I have no place to store my crops.'

This man was only concerned with wealth. One of his primary mistakes was believing that the abundant goods with which he had been blessed belonged to him. He didn't bother to seek God's guidance on what he should do with this bumper crop. God called him a fool, because this man thought *things* were enough to satisfy him.

Luke 12

> *19. 'And I'll say to myself, "You have plenty of good things laid up for many years. Take life easy: eat, drink and be merry."*
> *20. "But God said to him, 'You fool! This very night your life will be demanded from you. Then who will get what you have prepared for yourself?'*

Another mistake this man made was that he planned for the temporary, but not for the eternal. You can't join Jesus, hanging onto the "stuff" of this life. In verse 21, Jesus sums it all up:

Luke 12

21. "This is how it will be with anyone who stores up things for himself but is not rich toward God."

Treasure in Heaven lasts forever. The fool thought he had plenty of time and that his wealth put him in control of his future.

One of Satan's favorite deceptions is, "You have plenty of time." The rich man in Luke 12 thought he had time to eat, drink, and be merry, to live out his life in his own way without God. He was wrong. He didn't even get to see the next sunrise. The flowers for his funeral were already in full bloom.

How foolish to know that you need to return to God and refuse to do it, especially when returning to God is the only hope you have. Unless America returns, we will continue to face the measured steps of exposure until that exposure culminates in our destruction. A return to God is our only hope. Only then can we return to being the light of the world we were meant to be.

We should make it our fervent prayer that America will return to God. That return must begin where the exposure began, at the house of God. In 2 Chronicles we read:

2 Chronicles 7:14

"If My people, who are called by My name [that is God's people], *will humble themselves and pray and seek My face and turn from their wicked ways, then I will hear from heaven, and will forgive their sin and will heal their land."*

In other words, if God's people will lead the way in bringing their land—their nation—to God, then God can halt the exposure that nation is facing, and He can heal that land. However, if the nation refuses to join God's people in returning to God, He will still bless those who surrender to Him. God will bless the people who come to Him with eternal life and call them to fulfill the purpose He has for them. A person's fate need not be tied to the fate of an unbroken nation.

> *God will still bless those who surrender to Him.*

Not only will God give us a purpose, but He will also prepare a home for us in heaven when we surrender to Him. The Holy Spirit urges each of us to confess Jesus Christ as our Lord and Savior. Otherwise, we will face the judgment of God. There is an urgency about this decision, because there is *not* plenty of time when you are living in a nation exposed.

Indicator Two: Escapism

People who live in an exposed nation develop an obsession to escape reality and end up leading very distracted lives.

Isaiah 5

11. Woe to those who rise early in the morning to run after their drinks, who stay up late at night till they are inflamed with wine.
12. They have harps and lyres at their banquets, tambourines and flutes and wine, but they have no regard for the deeds of the Lord, no respect for the work of His hands.

The second indication that a nation has been allowed by God to become exposed is that it will become a nation distracted. Escape from reality becomes the predominate lifestyle, and is characterized by substance abuse and a preoccupation with entertainment and the distractions they both allow.

Illegal drug use first exploded on the scene in our nation, in a noticeable way, in conjunction with the rebellious 1960s. While levels of substance abuse have risen and fallen since the 1960s, the first decade of 2000 was marked by an increase in the use of illegal drugs in America from the lower levels of 1992. America, in 2010, was 4 percent of the world population, but they consumed two-thirds of the world's illegal drugs.[46] Substance abuse and addiction cost federal, state, and local governments almost a half-trillion dollars in 2005.[47] Two million full time college students, our brightest and best, met the medical criteria for substance abuse and dependence in 2007, the latest year for which these statistics were available.[48]

According to Isaiah, this escapist approach to life, with a heavy dependence on substances, becomes the norm in the nation that has moved into the second step of exposure. Many of the people in a nation exposed live their lives in a stupor, whether induced by alcohol, illegal drugs, or misuse of prescription medication. Combine the substance abuse with music and parties (their *banquets*) and no better definition of an escapist way of life can be found. What happens to a nation that persists in this distracted lifestyle?

> *Many live their lives in a stupor.*

God says that nation eventually deteriorates to such a low level that "... they have no regard for the deeds of the Lord, no respect for the work of his hands" (Is. 5:12). The focus of their lives has degenerated to withdrawing from reality into a fantasy world. They can't see God at work because they are so distracted, and even if they could see Him at work, they would still, because of their rebellion, refuse to give Him the respect He is due. If it feels good and it doesn't hurt anyone, "Let's do it!" I believe this is one of the most apt descriptions you can find anywhere for the mentality adopted by our nation.

Several years ago, after our nation had moved into this second step of exposure and begun its descent into escapism, the rock star Madonna appeared on HBO in the highest rated original program in the network's history, to date. She used obscene words that had been barred from public airways and simulated sexual acts on a bed on stage. To add insult to injury, HBO aired it during prime time on Sunday when many millions of children were watching. What surprised HBO officials the most? The fact that so few parents objected. In less than twenty years after our nation had moved into this second step of exposure, we readily accepted those things that had previously shocked us. We were numb to the moral deterioration occurring around us.

Is it any wonder that, in the first thirty years after moving into the second step of exposure, our nation saw premarital sex increase 200 percent among teenagers? Teenage pregnancy increased 400 percent, and teenage suicides increased 400 percent. Sexually transmitted diseases rose 200 percent among our youth.[49] We are living in a nation exposed. Isaiah goes on to explain what happens in a nation that is exposed and numbed as it embraces the escapist mentality.

Isaiah 5

13. Therefore my people will go into exile for lack of understanding: their men of rank will die of hunger and their masses will be parched with thirst.

God's people had been captured by this lifestyle of escapism. They had chosen to live their numbed, distracted lifestyle because they had no understanding of God. They had no respect for the deeds of God.

The nation had lost its heroes. It had no honorable men of rank to lead it. They had abandoned God, therefore, they could not continue to lead. The people no longer had their role models to lift them and inspire them to do good.

> *There are few heroes or honorable men in an exposed nation.*

The presence of the Spirit of God had been withdrawn from their nation, and God's hedge around them had been removed. They were completely exposed to the world around them.

There are few heroes or honorable men in an exposed nation. A president of our nation used his power to seduce a young woman in the Oval Office, and people accepted it. The people of our nation were so self-centered and so numbed by their escapist mentality that very little indignation was displayed. The moral fiber of our nation continued unraveling while our "men of rank" starved for greater attention, and "the masses" were thirsty for something to distract them from their desire for God.

People are born with three very basic desires or cravings: The *need to believe* in something that is true, the *need to become* by doing something worthwhile, and the *need to belong* by loving and being loved. Ultimately, these needs are only met when we live our lives in close proximity to the God who created us.

When we join our nation in refusing to return to God, we must look for substitutes to fill these longings in our souls; we must escape. America has become a nation of people looking for substitutes to meet the deepest desires of their hearts, desires that only God can meet. Unless we return to God, those soul desires will go unmet, because no substitute can do for us what only God can do. We must return to God or die of exposure.

Isaiah continues by describing what eventually happens to those people who are living the escapist mentality with no understanding that God alone can satisfy the cravings of their souls.

Isaiah 5

14. Therefore the grave enlarges its appetite and opens its mouth without limit; into it will descend their nobles and masses with all their brawlers and revelers.

What happens to those living in a nation exposed, who insist on embracing the escapist mentality? In short, they die. They go to the grave, the nobles and masses alike. No one is exempt. This lifestyle of distraction, of escapism, comes to an end as they realize it is too late to return to the God they have abandoned. They are "brought low" and "humbled" as they face living forever with their unfilled desires, exiled forever from the only One who can satisfy the

71

longings of their hearts. They will get their wish; they will escape from God forever. Isaiah states:

Isaiah 5

15. So man will be brought low and mankind humbled, the eyes of the arrogant humbled.
16. But the Lord Almighty will be exalted by His justice, and the holy God will show Himself holy by His righteousness.

Those who refused to return to God will be humbled. Those who sought to escape reality will face it because God will show justice. He is righteous. When He deals with the nation exposed, whatever He does will be right. He will exercise justice and set right all the wrong that has been done. But what will happen to the nation that has been left behind by its humbled citizens?

Isaiah 5

17. Then sheep will graze as in their own pasture; lambs will feed among the ruins of the rich.

Strangers move in and take over the nation that is exposed and steal that nation's prosperity. It is left in ruins, nothing more than a pasture for sheep to graze. In the time of Isaiah, the strangers who came in were from Babylon. Who will be the strangers that take over America if we do not return to God?

Indicator Three: Arrogance Toward God

There is a third indicator that a nation is facing the second step of exposure. It is arrogance toward God. Isaiah says of this third indicator:

Isaiah 5

18. Woe to those who draw sin along with cords of deceit. And wickedness as with cart ropes,

This is a picture of a person harnessed to a wagonload of sin, dragging their sin wherever they go. And while that sin may be a burden, they are not really as aware of that burden as they are of showing that sin off. There is a defiant attitude. They would rather embrace their sin than God. Notice what Isaiah says about their attitude toward God.

Isaiah 5

19. To those who say, "Let God hurry, let him hasten his work so we may see it. Let it approach, let the plan of the Holy One of Israel come, so we may know it."

They parade their sin out into the public arena. They shake their fists toward heaven and say, "If you don't like it God, let's see you do something about it." This is nothing more than a brash campaign of arrogance toward God. When a nation is exposed, sin is hauled out and freely displayed for everyone to see.

This sin leads naturally into a profane defiance of God that shakes its fist toward heaven and states, "I dare you to do something about my sin, God." Our society has certainly demonstrated an arrogant opposition to God. We teach our children that the human race evolved; that God had nothing to do with it. We tell our children that it is wrong for them to pray in school.

> *We tell our children that it is wrong for them to pray in school.*

I am convinced that America moved into the second step of exposure during the 1960s as a direct result of our open defiance of God. It was on June 25, 1962, that the Supreme Court ruled in the *Engel v. Vitale* case, disallowing students to use the following simple prayer in the public schools of our nation:

> Almighty God, we acknowledge our dependence upon Thee and beg Thy blessing upon us, our parents, our teachers, and our country.[50]

The 1962 *Engel v. Vitale* case, removing voluntary student prayer, was a watershed case. It was a turning point for this nation. This decision was made by the court without any previous precedent, either legal or historical.[51]

At that point, I believe God removed the hedge of protection around America. After 1962, violent crime rose 332 percent in twenty years.[52] This explosion of violence gave every indication that we had no intention of returning to God, so God removed His hedge of protection from our nation. We had moved into the second step of exposure. A Department of Labor study comparing productivity among twelve manufacturing countries revealed that the United States showed the largest productivity decline of the major industrial nations, beginning in 1962.[53]

America had moved into the second stage of exposure as a result of our arrogance toward God, and our productivity decline gave evidence of the greed that accompanied our refusal to return to God. This defiance of God began to permeate every part of our national life, including those things Americans relied on to distract them and to fuel their insatiable thirst to escape.

Even our art became a flagrant defiance of God. Several years ago, a so-called artist took a cross of Christ and submerged it in a bottle of his own urine and called it "art." He gave it a name so vulgar it doesn't bear repeating. Another artist depicted Jesus as an addict shooting himself up with heroine. If that's not hauling your sin out into the public arena, I don't know what is.

To add insult to injury, American's tax money paid for this so-called art. Each one of those artists received fifteen thousand dollars of American's tax money through the National Endowment for the Arts. We have become a nation that counts its arrogance of God as art.

When a nation of people refuses to return to God, the cycle of return and renewal is broken. God immediately moves, as He did with America in the 1950s, to remind that nation of the benefits it enjoys because of its relationship with Him. The groundwork of exposure has been laid. If that nation refuses at that point to return to God, it will be indicated by a radical rise in violence. God, with a broken heart, then removes His hand of protection from that nation, leaving it exposed to the political and natural world. The second step of exposure begins. Once again, the nation can choose: Return to God or continue living exposed.

If the nation chooses to refuse to return to God, its exposed existence will become evident in several ways. Greed and escapism will become obvious in the life of the nation. One of the most recognizable attitudes to emerge and gain strength in the exposed nation will be a defiant, arrogant attitude toward God.

America has obviously refused to return to God. Throughout the decades leading to the new millennium, our defiance toward God and the attempts to extricate Him from all aspects of our national life have grown in intensity. The first decade of 2000 was marked by attempts to have "In God We Trust" removed from America's coins and the phrase "Under God" removed from its pledge of allegiance. How arrogant.

We dare God to do something about it. Well, He has! We are living in a nation exposed. When a nation profanes the name of God in open arrogance, it is already exposed. The hedge of protection is gone.

> *We dare God to do something about it.*

Sinclair Lewis was one of the world's greatest playwrights at the pinnacle of his literary

77

career. Having won the Pulitzer Prize, he decided, in arrogant defiance against God, that he would write an outright attack against Christianity. So, in 1927, he wrote the popular *Elmer Gantry*, attacking God and Christianity. Critics in the American literary and entertainment fields revered his book and the subsequent movie. Both the book and the movie were widely applauded by the general public.

Sinclair Lewis popularized many of the heretical ideas of the 1920s that caused America to refuse to return to God. Lewis eventually became an alcoholic and died in anonymity. However, he had already contributed greatly toward the erosion of America's confidence in God and the church. Sinclair Lewis reaped the consequences of a life lived in arrogance toward God, and so will America, unless we return to God.

Indicator Four: Confusion of Good and Evil

When a nation is exposed, its defiance of God is seen by its open display of its sin. However, there is a fourth evidence that a nation is facing the second step of exposure. It is a confusion of good and evil.

Isaiah 5

*20. Woe to those who call evil good,
and good evil,
who put darkness for light, and light
for darkness,
who put bitter for sweet, and sweet
for bitter.*

A nation exposed starts evaluating things in reverse. What was wrong suddenly becomes right, and what was right suddenly becomes wrong. The entire value system is reversed.

America's changing view of marriage is a good barometer to indicate our confusion about what is right and what is wrong. There was a time in our nation, not very long ago, that we honored marriage and dishonored sex outside of marriage. Now, premarital sex is considered normal, and marriage for an extended period is considered abnormal.

In the years following the 1960s, the number of unmarried couples living together rose twelve-fold from 430 thousand in 1960 to 5.4 million in 2005[54] in our nation. The number of people getting married in America is declining, and for those getting married, they are less likely to stay married in America than in any other developed nation.[55] Even public opinion about the importance of marriage is slipping in

79

America. Sadly, more than eight out of ten couples who live together will break up either before the wedding or afterward in divorce. [56] Couples who do marry after living together are 50 percent more likely to divorce than those who did not. [57] We even view our children differently. Since 1976, child abuse has increased 240 percent, and sexual assault on children is up 2,300 percent.[58]

Our children are paying the price for our confusion of right and wrong. Children of cohabiting parents are ten times more likely to be sexually abused by a step parent, three times as likely to get expelled from school or become pregnant as a teenager, and twenty-two times more likely to be incarcerated. [59]

The American Pediatric Association published a report, just prior to the first decade of the 2000s, concluding that child molestation with "willing" children may not be harmful and may, in some cases, even be beneficial.[60] We have become a nation so confused that we don't understand the difference between good and evil any more.

How can we justify killing our children and allowing others to do the same? Are we really any better than the butchers of Auschwitz when we have murdered four times more people through abortions than the Nazis killed in the holocaust? Our prison population is growing at an alarming rate. We can't build prisons fast enough to cope with our confused principles.

A write-in survey by *U.S.A. Weekend* of an estimated 126 thousand kids, ages thirteen to eighteen, showed that many teens see nothing wrong with cheating on exams, stealing from employers, or keeping money that isn't theirs.[61] Our young people have no sense of right and wrong.

God has removed His hedge of protection from us as part of the exposure. The result of God removing His hedge of protection from a nation is strongly addressed in the Bible in the book of Romans.

Romans 1

26. Because of this, God gave them over to shameful lusts. Even their women exchanged natural relations for unnatural ones.
27. In the same way the men also abandoned natural relations with women and were inflamed with lust for one another. Men committed indecent acts with other men, and received in themselves the due penalty for their perversion.

This activity is all too prevalent in America today. Those who embrace the homosexual lifestyle have preferred not to have any knowledge of God. "God gave them over" is another way of saying that God removed His hand of protection from the people who lived and accepted the "unnatural" lifestyle. The nation that accepts homosexuality as an alternative lifestyle is a nation exposed. The Scripture further explains that the nation was given over to a mind unable to distinguish right from wrong.

Romans 1

28. Furthermore, since they did not think it worthwhile to retain the knowledge of God, He gave them over to a depraved mind, to do what ought not to be done.

The confusion of right and wrong that occurs in a nation that God allows to be exposed is seen in the emergence of radical, activist homosexuals. When you see homosexuals marching in the street and their lifestyle vigorously defended by that nation, then it is a sure sign that nation has already experienced the removal of God's hedge of protection and has proceeded well into the second step of exposure.

On June 11, 1999, President Clinton issued a proclamation:

> By virtue of the authority vested in me by the Constitution and Laws of the United States, I do hereby proclaim June of 1999, as Gay and Lesbian Pride Month. I encourage all Americans to observe this month with appropriate programs.[62]

The Bush administration appointed an activist homosexual as an ambassador to represent this nation in a foreign country. The ambassador took his live-in partner with him to the ambassador's home.

A dramatic shift has taken place in recent years regarding the attitude of Americans toward homosexuality and same sex marriage. A *Washington Post*/ABC poll in April 2009 reported, for the first time in the history of our nation, more Americans say they support same sex marriage (49 percent) than oppose it (46 percent), with 5 percent remaining neutral.[63] Several prominent sociologists are predicting that same sex marriages will soon be legal nationwide. [64]

In 1982, Gallup distinguished American's personal feelings about homosexuality from their opinions about its legality by asking the question: "Do you feel that homosexuality should be considered an acceptable alternative lifestyle or not?" At that time, just 34 percent of Americans polled said yes. In 2003, when the same question was asked, 54 percent of Americans responded that homosexuality should be considered an acceptable alternative lifestyle.[65]

Homosexuality continues to gain widespread acceptance in our nation as those who would dare challenge the morality of the homosexual lifestyle are labeled homophobic and ostracized by the media and entertainment elite of our nation. The rapid defense of the homosexual lifestyle in America is one of the surest signs that God has removed His hand of protection from America and given it over to a mind incapable of telling right from wrong or good from evil. We have refused to return to God, therefore, we have no moral foundation to decipher what is right from what is wrong.

Secretary of State in the Bush administration, Colin Powell, appeared on MTV in the first decade of 2000 and told young people to use condoms for protection, totally disregarding the findings of the National Institute of Health, that condoms do not provide adequate protection. Why are we so confused? Because God has removed His hedge of protection from this nation. We are an exposed people.

Indicator Five: Truth Replaced By Personal Opinion

There is a fifth indication that a nation is well into the second step of exposure—when truth is replaced by personal opinion as the standard that shapes perception. When the opinions of men become a greater virtue than truth, that nation is already experiencing the second stage of exposure.

Isaiah continues his discussion of a nation in the second stage of exposure:

Isaiah 5

21. Woe to those who are wise in their own eyes, and clever in their own sight!

In other words, everyone interprets truth in his or her own way. They operate by their own opinion. Self-centered, egotistical, radical individualism becomes a greater virtue than truth. There is no absolute authority that can be appealed to in a nation that has abandoned truth as its standard. You can no longer claim that one opinion is more valid

> *You can no longer claim that one opinion is more valid than another opinion.*

than another opinion. "I am right in my own eyes, and that is all that really matters," becomes the mind-set of the people in an exposed nation.

In this scenario, there is no truth by which to test opinion. The primary virtue in such a culture becomes tolerance, espousing the idea that we should tolerate all viewpoints because all viewpoints are equally valid. If you are doing something wrong, I can't call it wrong because, if it feels good to you and it is right in your eyes, it's okay.

During a meeting of college educators at Harvard University in 1987, President Frank Rhodes of Cornell University was discussing educational reforms, suggesting it was time for universities to pay "real and sustained attention to students' intellectual and moral well-being." Immediately, one student stood and demanded indignantly, "Who is going to do the instructing? Whose morality are we going to follow?" The audience applauded thunderously, affirming that the issue was settled because the student had asked an unanswerable question. President Rhodes sat down, unable to respond.[66] This affront by the angry student would have been easily handled in previous generations by appealing to the truth taught in Scripture, the basis of morality for centuries in the civilized world.

George Washington, after serving two terms as President of the United States, stated in his farewell address to the nation, the essential connection between morality and national survival:

> Whatever may be conceded to the influence of refined education on minds of peculiar structure, reason and experience both forbid us to expect that national morality can prevail in exclusion of religious principle (truth). It is substantially true that virtue of morality is a necessary spring of popular government.[67]

Washington recognized that no nation can survive once it abandons truth as the basis for national morality–a truth that is drawn from a source independent of personal opinion. Without that morality, a nation falls into disarray, exposed to the false ideas and philosophies of those around it. It becomes a nation adrift with a people exposed.

America no longer accepts truth as the standard for moral considerations. This erosion of our acceptance of truth, independent of our reasoning and experience, began with our acceptance of Nietzsche's philosophy that God

> *America no longer accepts truth as the standard for moral considerations.*

was inconsequential to our existence, and therefore, there was no standard of truth on which to base our lives. The keystone to Nietzsche's thoughts on truth is his 1873 unpublished essay, "On Truth and Lies in a Non-moral Sense." In this essay, Nietzsche rejects the idea of a universal constant of absolute truth and asserts that arbitrariness defines the human experience.[68] Drawing from, and agreeing that there was no guiding constant or truth, Karl Marx was among the early proponents of the premise that truth is socially constructed, and thus, truth becomes the consensus of the group or mob. Truth becomes whatever is agreed upon by a specific group.[69]

At the turn of the century, John Dewey, whose theories exerted a tremendous influence on education thought and theories in the American Educational System, continued the evolution of thought on truth by asserting that, since truth could be agreed upon by a specific group, it could be refined, refuted, and changed by that group or by a community of inquirers.[70]

Agreeably, the evolution of thought in America regarding truth has been oversimplified in this presentation. However, once the existence of truth independent of human reasoning and experience was rejected, the door was opened for extended and multiple speculations about what truth may or may not be. Our nation first began to embrace the idea that there was no constant truth guiding the universe, as asserted by Nietzsche, in the 1920s.

While Americans still clung to their belief in God, the stage had been set for them to start the process of removing God from the daily life of the nation. Americans started living as if God was dead. It was a simple matter for Americans to then embrace the Marxist philosophy that truth was whatever happened to be agreed upon by a specific group.

This radical departure from the acceptance of God as the Determiner of all truth, thus making truth subject to the human experience, began to take hold in our nation in the 1920s and gave rise to the postmodern worldview. While there are several branches of post modernism, the Postmodernist worldview, which sees truth as socially constructed, arising from Marxism, began to dominate thought in America.[71] This solidified our refusal to return to God.

> *Americans started living as if God was dead.*

As Americans, we are radical individualists, and the concept that truth was arrived at as a consensus by a specific group did not sit well with us. The postmodern thought process, in America, began to transition from the consensus of the group being the determining factor in arriving at truth, to the individual's opinion being the final authority regarding truth. While this approach to the determination of truth is self-referential, it is also inconsistent. Opinions differ. Postmodern thought embraces this inconsistency by seeking to legitimatize the individual's right to assert their opinion; therefore, what is truth to me is not necessarily truth to you.

Truth is defined, in postmodern America, as whatever my experience or reasoning tells me about my situation. My opinion about my situation then becomes the determining factor in the choices and decisions I make, putting me in direct conflict with others, whose opinion about our shared situation may be different. The result is chaos–a culture of independently opinionated people who have no external source to rely upon to determine what is true, and thus, what is real.

However, there is not only cultural chaos, but individual confusion. What is true to me today, in my current situation, may not be true to me tomorrow in a similar, nearly identical, situation. I am left conflicted. Truth has become relative, subjective. There is no larger story that makes sense of reality. There is only a collection of disjointed stories in which we live, trying to make sense of our experience, but unable to determine what is real and what is not.

Americans found themselves on this slippery slope as they began to incorporate the radical ideas of Nietzsche, Marx, Dewey, and others into the educational system of America, beginning in the 1920s and 1930s.

As Abraham Lincoln stated, "The philosophy of the classroom today will be the philosophy of government tomorrow."[72] These ideas were not only prominent in the education of our children, and thus, in the next generation, our government, but in our individual thinking as well.

In January 2000, a Barna research poll showed that only 38 percent of adult Americans believed that absolute truth even existed, leaving 62 percent of the adult population of our nation embracing opinion over truth. By November 2001, another Barna poll showed that American adults believing in the existence of truth independent of their opinion had dropped almost in half to 22 percent.[73] At the beginning of the first decade of the 2000s, 78 percent of the adults in America did not believe that truth existed.

America shows no evidence of reversing this radical trend of making personal opinion, rather than truth, the determining factor in the choices and decisions of our lives. Since individuals and situations change readily,

> *Seventy-eight percent of adults in America did not believe that truth existed.*

there is, therefore, no standard of morality when opinion is elevated to this point.

Chuck Colson stated, "Today... few educators–or any other leaders who shape public attitudes–have the audacity to challenge the prevailing assumption that there is no morally binding objective source of authority or truth above the individual."[74]

When man's opinions and his perceptions, rather than God's, become the controlling factor in a nation, people do whatever they want. They have abandoned God's leadership for that of their own opinion. A nation dominated by the opinions of its people, and not by God's truth, is a nation living exposed.

Indicator Six: Political Corruption

There is a sixth indicator that a nation is experiencing the removal of God's protection: it is political corruption.

Isaiah 5

22. Woe to those who are heroes at drinking wine and champions at mixing drinks,
23. who acquit the guilty for a bribe, but deny justice to the innocent.

Here, the evidence of exposure is found in those persons in leadership roles who have influence, authority, or power within the nation, whose decisions significantly affect the lives of others. The Scripture here tells us that political officials and leaders, for a bribe, will set a guilty man free and deny justice to the innocent.

These verses address both the personal and official conduct of those who are charged with the responsibility of providing leadership to the nation being exposed. Personally, they are "heroes at drinking wine and champions at mixing drinks." Their personal conduct is dominated by substances that not only alter their reasoning ability, but undermine their capacity for making moral decisions.

Officially, their corruption is demonstrated by their undermining of the rule of law, accepting bribes from the guilty and denying justice to the innocent. In short, they manipulate the system for their own advantage, disregarding the impact their actions have on the moral fiber of the nation, or the personal lives of those they victimize as they promote their own selfish agenda.

Judge Edith Jones of the U.S. Court of Appeals for the 5th Circuit told the Federalist Society of Harvard Law School that the American legal system has been corrupted almost beyond recognition. She explained:

> Lawyers' private morality has definite public consequences. Their misbehavior feeds on itself, encouraging disrespect and debasement of the rule of law as the public become encouraged to press their own advantage in a system they perceive as manipulatable. [75]

She went on to state that the first one hundred years of American lawyers were trained on Blackstone, who asserted that:

> The law of nature, dictated by God Himself is binding….No human laws are of any validity if contrary to this; and such of them as are valid derive all force and all their authority from this original.[76]

As a nation distances itself from God and His laws, not only does the moral fiber of that nation begin to deteriorate, but the rule of law is eroded from the life of the people of that nation. What is morally right is routinely sacrificed for political expediency. Judge Jones stated:

> Having lost sight of the moral and religious foundations of the rule of law, we are vulnerable to the destruction

of our freedom, our equality before the law, and our self-respect…. The answer is a recovery of the moral principle.[77]

The only possible hope of recovery for America is a return to God and a re-embracing of His laws as the foundation of any sustainable rule of law. Once a nation moves into the second step of exposure and the rule of law begins to disintegrate in the nation, as a whole, political corruption becomes prevalent. From 1976 to the 1990s, the prosecution of public officials for corruption in America rose over 450 percent.[78] The 1990s were marked by only the second attempt in our nation's history to impeach a sitting president, who was charged with perjury, a blatant disregard for the rule of law for personal expediency.

> *The rule of law begins to disintegrate in the nation.*

The first decade of the new millennium saw an explosion of corruption in our nation. In 2004, Connecticut Governor John Rowland's administration faced the worst public corruption scandal in the state's history. Three Connecticut mayors and the state treasurer were sent to prison. The governor's former deputy chief of staff pled guilty to accepting gold coins in return for government contracts. He reportedly buried the coins in his backyard.

Governor Rowland confessed that he allowed private corporations to renovate his personal cottage in exchange for certain favors.[79] The governor of Illinois was indicted and impeached for attempting to sell the Senate Seat vacated by President Obama when he was elected to the presidency.

After campaigning on a platform of returning his state to a renewed moral foundation of family values, the governor of New York was forced to resign for engaging the services of several prostitutes. His successor, while admitting his own moral indiscretions, was soon facing questions about his unethical behavior. The Governor of South Carolina, once touted as a potential presidential candidate for his party, abandoned his post for several days and issued a statement that was inaccurate about his location. He was actually with his mistress in Argentina, and, it was later discovered, had taken frequent trips to rendezvous with her while claiming to be on state business. He refused to resign his position and survived an impeachment attempt.

Three consecutive insurance commissioners in the state of Louisiana, and the agricultural commissioner were indicted for receiving bribes during the first decade of 2000.[80]

John Edwards, former Senator from North Carolina and the 2004 Democratic candidate for Vice President, was a viable candidate for President in 2008 until rumors began to surface about possible indiscretions on his part. In 2010, Edwards confessed that he had an affair with aide Rielle Hunter and fathered a child out of wedlock while his wife was battling metastasized breast cancer.

Former Vice President Al Gore and his wife, Tipper, announced in June 2010, that their marriage of forty years was ending. Marriage for some of our national political figures has become an "inconvenient truth."

The District of Columbia, the seat of our national government, has been determined to be "the most corrupt political entity in the nation," managing to accumulate 453 public corruption convictions over a ten-year period.[81] Compare that to Kentucky, which was worse than forty-two other states, with 188 convictions of public officials by federal prosecutors over a ten-year period.[82] One prominent former mayor of Washington, D. C. was publicly waging an anti-drug campaign while he was privately addicted to cocaine.

It is the judiciary in America that is charged with the responsibility of guarding the rule of law. Isaiah says that it is in the judiciary that corruption is most evident in a nation exposed, and it is because of the corrupt judiciary that the rule of law collapses. When judges are corrupt, the rule of law is lost and personal expediency rules the day. The corruption of the judiciary in America begins at the federal level and permeates our legal system all the way to the local level.

Twelve federal judges wield virtually exclusive power over misconduct investigations of more than two thousand of their fellow federal judges, though some of these powerful judges have, themselves, been accused of unethical behavior according to a study by the Houston Chronicle.[83]

At least four current or former Chief Circuit Judges have been the subject of high profile complaints. One of these federal judges posted photos of naked women painted to look like cows on his website! Another judge manipulated the outcome of a vote in a death penalty case.

Not one federal judge faced formal discipline.[84] In fact, there were more than six thousand complaints filed against federal judges in the first decade of the new millennium. In seven circuits, supervising judges took no disciplinary action. In other words, not a single federal judge faced any disciplinary action in twenty-nine states in the first ten years of 2000, despite thousands of complaints.[85]

Local courts have fared no better as the prevailing corruption has permeated our legal system over the last several decades. The FBI's *Operation Greylord* investigation revealed extensive corruption in the courts of Cook County, Illinois in the 1980s.[86] Fifteen judges and attorneys in the Youngstown, Ohio area were convicted of federal crimes between 1997 and 2000.[87] A *Washington Post* study, published in 2000, detailed wide-spread misconduct in the Hillsborough, Florida court system.[88]

The first decade of 2000 was marred by the revelation of systemic corruption in the judiciary in Brooklyn, New York.[89] One Brooklyn judge was convicted of soliciting bribes and was sentenced to prison.[90] Another judge was charged with rigging a divorce.[91] At least fourteen Brooklyn judges faced ethical or criminal investigations, [92] and the district attorney continues to uncover still more allegations.[93]

There is corruption almost everywhere. The few good men and women in politics and leadership in our nation stand out in sharp contrast to those who have abandoned the moral directives upon which the laws of this nation were founded. Judge Edith Jones, in her address to the Harvard Law School, quoted Professor Harold Breman:

> *There is corruption almost everywhere.*

> The traditional Western beliefs in the structural integrity of the law, its on-goingness, its religious roots, its transcendent qualities, are disappearing not only from the minds of law teachers and law students, but also from the consciousness of the vast majority of citizens, the people as a whole.... The law, itself, is becoming more fragmented, more subjective, geared more to expediency and less to morality.[94]

It is obvious that we, as a people, have moved far along in the second step of exposure. All of the indicators are there that God has removed His protection from us, and we have become a nation exposed. We have refused to return to God and experience the Spiritual renewal we so desperately need, and God wants us to have.

The pattern of: *a financial crisis, a return to God, a spiritual renewal, followed by a war, and prosperity, only to repeat the pattern*, is the means that God interacts with any nation desiring His protection. We as a nation left that pattern in the 1920s. In spite of the hardships of the 1930s and the bloodshed of the 1940s, we refused to return to God. As a result of our rebellion against God and our refusal to return to

Him, God moved to get America's attention by allowing us to become a nation exposed.

> **1920s**—The cycle of return and renewal is broken.
> **1930s and 1940s**—There is hardship and bloodshed, but America does not return to God.
> **1950s**—**The First Stage of Exposure**: God reminds America of the benefits it enjoys because of its relationship with Him.

If the nation refuses to return to God at this point, it will be indicated by a rapid rise in violence, which happened in America. We refused to return to God.

> **1962**—**The Second Step of Exposure:** God, with a broken heart, removes His protection from America.

In our arrogance, we still refused to return to Him. Our nation moved further along in the second stage of exposure. Our exposed existence has become obvious in the life of our nation in several ways:

Indicator 1: Greed
The mentality of the people of the nation exposed is to add "house to house."

Indicator 2: Escapism
The preoccupation of the people in an exposed nation is to escape reality, so they embrace whatever substance or activity offers them that escape.

Indicator 3: Arrogance Toward God
There is a concerted effort by the citizens of a nation being exposed to remove all reference to God and to arrogantly put their sin on display.

Indicator 4: Confusion of Good and Evil
The people of a nation advancing through the second stage of exposure lose the capacity to tell right from wrong. The moral fiber of the nation unravels.

Indicator 5: Truth Replaced by Personal Opinion
The idea of a universal or absolute truth independent of human experience or reason is abandoned by the people in a nation exposed in favor of personal opinion.

Indicator 6: Political Corruption
The unraveling of the moral fiber of the nation exposed and the subsequent abandonment of truth as the standard for life and behavior result in the abandonment of the rule of law in the life of the nation. Expediency replaces morality and corruption becomes wide-spread.

To those who will open their eyes and see, it is obvious that these six indicators show that God has removed His protection from America. We are a nation exposed, and because we refused to return to God as the exposure deepened, God moved America into the third step of exposure.

Chapter Four

The Third Step of Exposure: God Releases the Nation's Punishment

I believe that God initiated the second step of exposure of America by removing His protection from our nation in 1962, as a direct result of the Supreme Court ruling, *Engel v. Vitale*, which denied students the opportunity of offering a simple prayer to God in the public schools of our nation. This ruling followed God's reminding the people of America of the prosperity the nation enjoyed because of its relationship with Him.

America's response to the many benefits we enjoyed because of our relationship with God was to tell our students they couldn't pray to Him in the schools of our nation. America's refusal to return to God after He had initiated this first step of exposure in the 1950s constituted rebellion on our part.

America had no intention of returning to God, so God moved us into the second step of exposure in 1962. The violence that became rampant in our nation during that time revealed that we were not returning to God. Our nation plunged headlong into the second step of exposure. Greed, escapism, and arrogance toward God, coupled with an inability to distinguish right from wrong, a replacement of truth by opinion, and widespread political corruption became the factors that shaped daily life in our nation.

As each of these characteristics intensified in America and actually began to define the people of our nation, it became obvious that the nation showed no intention of returning to God. God took action. He moved our nation into the third step of exposure. It is important to note that the factors that defined our people in the second step of exposure did not go away. They simply intensified, and will continue to do so.

Substantive changes in the nation's morality and people occur during the second step of exposure. In the third stage of exposure, the nation faces challenges from outside, challenges that are difficult for the exposed nation to handle because of the diminished morality of its people and its weakened condition. I am convinced that God took America into the third step of exposure by allowing our nation to face powerful external challenges that threaten our very existence. Isaiah describes how God exposed the sins of His own people as He moved the nation into the third step of exposure.

Isaiah 5

24. Therefore, as tongues of fire lick up straw and as dry grass sinks down in the flames, so their roots will decay and their flowers blow away like dust; for they have rejected the law of the Lord Almighty and spurned the word of the Holy One of Israel.

God uses the graphic picture of a fire that burns its way through a field, devouring everything in its path. The effectiveness of a nation that has moved into the third stage of exposure is lost. It is no more significant than straw or dry grass in a raging fire. It is rotten to its very roots, so that even those things that were once beautiful about the nation become ugly and dry as dust. America, the nation that offered freedom to those who could make it to her shores, blossomed with opportunity at one time. The freedom she offered was the flower of hope to many around the world. As America moved into the third stage of exposure, her offer of hope to the weary and tired people in our world diminished.

A nation in the third stage of exposure is not a very pretty sight. Why would God move a nation into the third step of exposure? He says that He does this to a nation that has "rejected the law of the LORD Almighty..." (Isaiah 5:24b).

Once God has demonstrated to a nation the extent of the blessings He has given them, with no corresponding expression of brokenness and appreciation from the nation, He then will remove the hedge of protection from that nation.

If that season of exposure does not bring that nation to return to Him, then God will release their punishment by allowing external challenges to assault the nation. God takes three specific actions when He moves a nation into the third step of exposure, all in an attempt to encourage the nation to return to Him:

Action One: God Exposes His Own People

How does God release the punishment of an exposed nation? He first begins with His own people–those who are charged with the responsibility of handling and presenting His Word. While we tend to blame secular America for causing God's exposure of our nation, the blame actually must be placed with God's people. Isaiah describes what this third stage of exposure looks like as God exposes the sins of His people.

Isaiah 5

25(a).Therefore the Lord's anger burns against His people; His hand is raised and He strikes them down.

The Lord is upset with His people as He continues to pursue exposure against a rebellious nation. His anger burns and He strikes them down.

The hope of America lies in God's people returning to God first. The Bible tells us that judgment must begin with the family of God.[95] God takes a nation into the third step of exposure by exposing the sins of His own people.

In 1988 we witnessed the collapse of two prominent ministers in our nation: Jim Bakker of *Praise the Lord* (PTL) fame and Jimmy Swaggert. Others subsequently fell or were exposed as charlatans. The number of prominent pastors across the nation who have been forced to resign in shame as their sin has been revealed has reached epidemic proportions.

> *God takes a nation into the third step of exposure by exposing the sins of His people.*

In 1986, Jimmy Swaggert

began attacking, on his own television program, fellow pastors Marvin Gorman and Jim Bakker. He exposed Gorman's affair with a member of Gorman's church and Jim Bakker's infidelity with Jessica Hahn during an out of state trip. These exposures received extensive media coverage, becoming the focus of the nation.[96]

Gorman, as a result of Swaggert's exposure of his affair, resigned the pastorate of the five thousand member First Assembly of God Church in New Orleans.[97] On March 19, 1987, following the revelation of a payoff to Jessica Hahn to keep secret the allegation that Jim Bakker had raped her, Bakker resigned from his ministry, PTL.[98] In retaliation against Swaggert's exposure of his affair, Marvin Gorman hired a private investigator to uncover Swaggert's adulterous activity with a prostitute.[99]

In 1988, Jim Bakker was indicted on eight counts of mail fraud, fifteen counts of wire fraud, and one count of conspiracy.[100] In 1988, after a trial in Charlotte, North Carolina, the jury found him guilty on all twenty-four counts, and Judge Robert Patten sentenced him to forty-five years in federal prison and a fine of $500 thousand.[101] His sentence was later reduced to the fine and eight years[102]

In February 1988, Swaggert was suspended for three months from his U. S. pulpit and given a two year rehabilitation period.[103]

The indictment of Jim Bakker and the public apology of Jimmy Swaggert, both in 1988, opened the floodgates regarding the exposure of the wrongs being committed by prominent ministries in our nation. I am convinced that it was at this point, in 1988, that God intensified the third step of exposure into which He had moved our nation by specifically exposing the sins of His own people, those charged with the responsibility of handling His Word.

The church and ministries in America entered into a time of unprecedented exposure in 1988 as corruption was revealed at all levels. Never in our history as a nation has the church and ministries associated with it faced such scrutiny and been found so lacking.

The following is only a partial list of the churches, pastors, and ministries whose sins have been exposed since God moved America into the third step of exposure:

1991

Mike Warnke – *Cornerstone Magazine*, in an investigation of Warnke's life and testimony, uncovered lies about the extent of his involvement with Satanism prior to his conversion to Christianity as well as evidence of fraud, deceit, and damaging information regarding his multiple marriages and affairs.[104]

Robert Tilton – An investigation of Tilton's ministry by Diane Sawyer and ABC News, aired on November 21, 1991 on ABC's *Prime Time Live*. They discovered that Tilton's ministry discarded prayer requests without reading them, collecting only the money and valuables sent by viewers contributing to his ministry's revenue of $80 million a year.[105]

Jimmy Swaggert – After his much publicized apology in 1988, California police caught Swaggert with another prostitute, Rosemary Garcia, in 1991. When she was asked why she was in the car with Swaggert, Rosemary responded, "He asked me for sex." [106]

1992

Morris Cerrullo – Once a partner in ministry with Mike Warnke, Cerrullo claimed a child cancer sufferer was healed. The girl died of cancer two months later. His claims of similar miraculous healings were proven false by a panel of doctors, and his fund-raising material was condemned as unethical for implying that money given to his ministry would result in family members becoming Christians.[107] Audrey Reynolds, a twenty-five year old epileptic, who was proclaimed healed by Cerrullo, drowned in her bath having abandoned her epileptic medication.[108]

1996

W.V. Grant – Grant was imprisoned for tax evasion in 1996. After his release, a television investigation found that he falsified claims of healing at a 2003 revival in Atlanta.[109]

1998

Henry Lyons – The former President of the National Baptist Convention, USA, Inc. was indicted by federal prosecutors for fraud, extortion, money laundering, conspiracy, and tax evasion.[110] He was sentenced to a total of five and a half years in prison for misappropriation of more than $4 million from the National Baptist Convention while he was its President. [111]

2000

John Paulk – In September 2000, John Paulk, leader of Focus on the Family's *Love Won Out Conference* and former Chairman of the Board for Exodus International North America, was photographed in a gay bar in Washington, D. C. and was accused of flirting with male patrons. Paulk, who claimed leaving homosexuality in his autobiography, *Not Afraid to Change*, at first denied being in the bar and was supported by Dr. James Dobson, President of Focus on the Family. Paulk later confessed to being in the bar. [112]

2002

Church Sex Scandals – While the scandal regarding sexual abuse of children by Catholic priests had broken earlier, it began to preoccupy the interest of the nation in 2002 and beyond. A great deal of attention was given to a survey done by the *Dallas Morning News*, claiming that two-thirds of the convicted bishops had allowed priests accused of sexual abuse to continue working.[113] A survey by the *New York Times* reported that 1.8 percent of all priests ordained from 1950 to 2001 have been accused of child sexual abuse.[114]

While the Catholic clergy seemed to be the primary focus of much of the interest regarding sexual misconduct, studies were also done which showed alarming trends regarding Protestant clergy. In 1984, a Fuller Seminary survey of 1200 ministers found that 20 percent of theologically conservative pastors admitted to some sexual contact outside of marriage with a church member. The figure climbed to over 40 percent for moderates, and 50 percent of liberal pastors confessed to similar activity.[115]

A 1990 study learned that 25 percent of pastors admitted to some sexual contact with a church member.[116] In 1992, a survey by *Leadership Magazine* found that 37 percent of ministers confessed to having been involved in "inappropriate sexual behavior" with a church member.[117] By 2001, it was estimated that about 20 percent of all ministers suffer from pornography and sexual addiction.[118]

A 2000 report to the Baptist General Convention in Texas stated, "The incidence of sexual abuse by clergy has reached 'horrific proportions.'" The report concluded, "The disturbing aspect of all research is that the rate of incidence for clergy exceeds the client-professional rate for physicians and psychologists."[119]

> *We are a nation of deteriorating morals.*

It would appear that God is exposing the sins of His people in unprecedented fashion. We are a nation of deteriorating morals in the third step of exposure.

2004

Paul Crouch – In September 2004, the *Los Angeles Times* published several articles questioning the fund-raising practices and financial accountability of the Trinity Broadcasting Network (TBN) whose founder and president is Paul Crouch. Also alleged in the article was the claim by a former ministry employee, Enoch Ford, that he had engaged in a homosexual affair with Crouch in the 1990s. TBN denied the allegations. In 2005, Ford submitted to and passed a lie detector test.[120]

2006

Lonnie Latham – Latham, senior pastor of the South Tulsa Baptist Church and a trustee of the Southern Baptist Convention Executive Committee was arrested in 2006 for "offering to engage in an act of lewdness" with a male undercover police officer. Latham admitted he had asked the officer for sex. An Oklahoma judge later dismissed the charges.[121]

Paul Barnes – Barnes, founder and senior minister of the twenty-one hundred member Grace Chapel Church in Douglas County, Colorado resigned on December 7, 2006 after confessing his homosexual activity to the church board.[122]

Kent Hovind – An American Baptist minister most noted for his creation science seminars, Hovind was charged in 2006 with falsely declaring bankruptcy, making threats against federal officials, filing false complaints, failing to get necessary building permits, and various tax-related charges. He is currently serving a ten year sentence following his conviction on five federal tax charges and related offenses.[123]

Ted Haggard – As president of the National Association of Evangelicals (NAE) from 2003 to November 2006 and pastor of the New Life Church in Colorado Springs, Colorado, Ted Haggard's admission of regularly visiting a male prostitute who also provided him with methamphetamine was one of the most shocking exposures of wrongdoing to many people associated with the Church in America. Haggard's high visibility as a prominent leader in evangelical circles gave him access to President George Bush as an adviser. Haggard resigned both his pastorate and the presidency of the NAE. In January 2009, Haggard admitted to a second homosexual relationship with a male church member and refused to respond to inquiries about other possible homosexual relationships.[124]

2007

Coy Privette – A prominent figure in North Carolina moral battles, Privette, a Baptist pastor and politician, was president of the Christian Action League and a member of the Executive Committee of the North Carolina Baptist State Convention. He resigned each of these positions following revelations that he had been charged on July 19, 2007 with six counts of aiding and abetting prostitution.[125]

Thomas Wesley Weeks, III – Weeks, who founded Global Outreach Ministries in 1997, married televangelist Juanita Bynum in 2002. They later divorced in 2008 after Weeks physically assaulted Bynum in a hotel parking lot on August 22, 2007.[126]

Earl Paulk – Paulk was the founder and senior pastor of Chapel Hill Harvester Church in Decatur, Georgia from 1960 until the 1990s. Several women from the congregation have claimed that Paulk had sexual relations with them. A number of these claims have proven correct. Donnie Earl Paulk, the current lead pastor of the church and nephew of Earl Paulk, had a court ordered DNA test in 2007 which proved that he was Earl's son, not his nephew. Earl and his sister-in-law had engaged in a sexual relationship that led to Donnie's birth.[127]

Richard Roberts – Son of the late televangelist Oral Roberts, Richard Roberts was forced to resign as president of Oral Roberts University on

November 23, 2007 for alleged improper use of university funds for political and personal purposes and improper use of university resources.[128]

Senate Probe – In 2007, Senator Chuck Grassley (R-IA) opened an investigation into the ministries of six televangelists. The probe looked into reports of lavish lifestyles by the individuals who led these ministries including huge mansions, private jets, marble commodes, Rolls Royces, Bentleys, and other expensive items paid for by television viewers who responded to the ministers' appeals for donations.[129] The six ministers under investigation are:

- **Kenneth Copeland and Gloria Copeland** of Kenneth Copeland Ministries of Newark, Texas
- **Creflo Dollar and Taffi Dollar** of World Changers Church International and Creflo Dollar Ministries of College Park, Georgia
- **Benny Hinn** of World Healing Center Church, Inc. and Benny Hinn Ministries of Grapevine, Texas
- **Eddie L. Long** of New Birth Missionary Baptist Church and Bishop Eddie Long Ministries of Lithonia, Georgia

- **Joyce Meyer and David Meyer** of Joyce Meyer Ministries of Fenton, Missouri
- **Paula White and ex-husband Randy White** of Without Walls International Church and Paula White Ministries of Tampa, Florida.[130]

The investigation is ongoing with differing levels of cooperation from the various ministries, including resistance from Kenneth Copeland and his ministry.[131]

2008

Joe Barron – One of forty ministers on staff at Prestonwood Baptist Church, Joe Barron was arrested on May 15, 2008 for solicitation of a minor. Barron drove from Dallas to Bryan, Texas to allegedly engage in sexual relations with a thirteen-year-old girl he had met online. The girl was actually an undercover law enforcement officer.[132] Baron was dismissed from the staff at Prestonwood Baptist Church which, with twenty-six thousand members, is one of the largest churches in America.

As a result of this arrest, the Survivors Network of Those Abused by Priests (SNAP) director, David Clohessy stated:

> Baptist officials, we believe, need to compile a thorough, online database of proven, admitted and credibly accused pedophile clergy, so that kids can be protected and parents can be warned.

SNAP has expanded its focus in recent years, giving attention to abuse by Baptist Pastors.[133]

Tony Alamo – On September 20, 2008, FBI agents raided Tony Alamo Christian Ministries headquarters following allegations of child pornography, physical abuse, sexual abuse, and under-age marriage.[134] In July 2009, Alamo was convicted on ten counts of transporting minors across state lines for sexual purposes, sexual assault, and other crimes. On November 13, 2009, Alamo was sentenced to the maximum punishment of 175 years in prison.[135]

Todd Bentley – Bentley became well known as the evangelist of the Lakeland Revival in Florida which began in April 2008. Bentley claimed that tens of thousands of people were healed at the revival, but an investigation conducted by ABC's *Nightline* in June 2008, could not find a single confirmed miracle. Bentley took a break from the meetings after the program was aired, but later returned. In August 2008, he left the meetings permanently when it was revealed that he was separating from his wife and was in a relationship with a member of his staff.[136]

2010

George Alan Rekers – Rekers, a far right Christian leader, was confronted and photographed at Miami International Airport returning from an overseas trip with a twenty-year-old gay male prostitute. Rekers has been an outspoken opponent of homosexuality and claimed that the young man was simply escorting him to carry his luggage due to Rekers' recent surgery. However, Rekers was seen carrying his own luggage when the two were spotted at the airport. Rekers, a Baptist minister and often recognized as a leading scholar for the Christian right wing, formed the Family Research Council with Dr. James Dobson in 1983.[137]

Benny Hinn – In 2007, Hinn's ministry became one of several nationwide ministries under investigation by the US Senate (see discussion–2007). On February 1, 2010, Hinn's wife, Suzanne, filed papers in Orange County, California Superior Court seeking a divorce, citing "irreconcilable differences." The couple has four children together.[138]

While this list is extensive, it is certainly not exhaustive. It focuses primarily on those churches and individuals that are noted for their national exposure, and it does not address those whose ministries are more local in nature. It is sobering to say the least. God is exposing the sins of those who claim to be His people, those who have been charged with the responsibility of representing Him to the nation.

A nation in the third step of exposure also experiences a dramatic loss of confidence by its people in those individuals who should be leading the nation to return to God. In a survey for the *Wall Street Journal* and NBC News, it was found that 64 percent of the public thought that Catholic priests frequently abused children.[139]

A 2007 study conducted by the Barna Group among sixteen to twenty-nine-year-olds found that only 3 percent of this group has favorable views of evangelicals and only 16 percent have a good impression of Christianity as a whole.[140] The most common perception is that present day Christianity is "anti-homosexual" with 91 percent of young non-Christians saying this phrase describes Christianity.[141]

A decided shift is occurring in the faith allegiances of Americans. Each emerging generation has a larger share of its people who are not Christians. There are more non-Christians in

America right now than at any time in our history, and unless we return to God as a nation, that same statement can be made in ensuing generations if America continues to exist.[142]

I am convinced that God intensified the third step of exposure that our nation was experiencing in 1988 as He set about to uncover the sins of His people. Removal of the hedge of protection around our nation did not produce a return to God from God's own people, so God released His punishment against America by divulging the sins of His people. Until God's people return to God, our land will not be healed. The exposure will continue.

2 Chronicles 7

14. "If My people, who are called by My name will humble themselves, and pray and seek My face, and turn from their wicked ways, then will I hear from heaven, and will forgive their sin and will heal their land."

Our land is not being healed because God's people have refused to repent and lead our nation to return to Him. God has taken action. He has moved America into the third step of exposure by exposing the sins of His own people. If God's people refuse to be broken over the wrongs in our own ranks, how will our nation ever be healed? How will it ever return to God?

Action Two: God Releases Natural Disasters

Isaiah continues his graphic picture of the actions that God takes as He moves a nation into the third step of exposure. He not only divulges the sins of His own people, but He unleashes a deluge of national disasters against the exposed nation.

> Isaiah 5
>
> *25(b). His hand is raised and He strikes them down.*
> *The mountains shake, and the dead bodies are like refuse in the streets.*
> *Yet for all this, His anger is not turned away, his Hand is still upraised.*

God causes natural disasters to take place.

God causes natural disasters to take place in the exposed nation. He shakes the nation, saying, "I want you to realize that you are facing exposure. Return to Me!" As

God exposes the sins of His own people in the third step of exposure, He will also release His punishment against a rebellious nation by allowing that nation to experience a series of natural disasters.

The uncovering of the sins of God's people and the release of exceptional natural disasters on a nation exposed occurs almost simultaneously. The "mountains shake" (v. 25) in the exposed nation, and the bodies of the residents of that nation will be strewn in the streets (v. 25).

God will continue to keep His hand "upraised" against the nation being exposed as He releases natural disasters to assault the nation. If America has moved into the third step of exposure, there should be a corresponding increase in natural disasters in our nation to authenticate this continuation of God's exposure of America.

NBC News, on May 4, 1999, reported that damages caused by natural disasters in the 1980s and 1990s in the United States were greater than any other period in history. Hurricanes accounted for $62 billion in damages during those two decades; tornadoes and floods, $48 billion in damages; droughts, $75 billion. In 1998, the damages caused by natural disasters in America were the highest in our history to that date.[143]

I believe that God moved our nation into the third step of exposure in 1985 as He unleashed natural disasters of unparalleled magnitude and intensity on our nation. The following disasters occurred in 1985 in America, marking a dramatic increase in natural disasters over previous years.

> *It was as if God were shaking the hills of San Francisco.*

From January 18 through 23, 1985, one hundred twenty three died in a cold wave in the eastern United States. On May 31, eighty-eight died in tornadoes across Pennsylvania and Ohio. On August 2, one-hundred-thirty-seven died in a plane crash caused by thunderstorms in Dallas, Texas. On September 2, four died and $543 million in damages occurred as Hurricane Alana slammed into the Mississippi coast.

Between October 22 and 29, eight died and $1 billion in damages were racked up by Hurricane Juan's attack against the Louisiana coast. On November 5, forty-five died in the worst floods ever in Maryland, Virginia, Pennsylvania, West Virginia, and North Carolina. On November 21 and 22, seven people died and another $1 billion in damages accrued as Hurricane Kate violently moved against the Florida and Georgia coasts.[144] Then suddenly, everything fell silent. For three years, there were no major natural disasters, neither was there a subsequent return to God.

In 1988, we watched the collapse of the ministries of Jim Bakker and Jimmy Swaggart. Did God's people lead America to return to God? No! America's response to God's merciful warnings was to release, in 1988, the blasphemous movie *The Last Temptation of Christ.*

Immediately following the release of this movie, there was a violent resurgence of natural disasters. During September 17 through 22, 1989, there were seventy-one deaths and $8 billion in damages as Hurricane Hugo devastated the South Carolina coast.

Then exactly one month after Hugo, on October 17, 1989, sixty-two deaths and $7 billion in damages resulted from the San Francisco earthquake.[145] This disaster occurred during the World Series when the eyes of the entire nation were focused on the Bay Area. It was as if God were shaking the hills of San Francisco and saying, "Wake up, America, before it's too late!"

Still there was no corresponding return to God. We went into another three-year waiting period from 1989 to 1992, when only a few regional disasters took place. Then the silence ended with a bang!

In August of 1992, Hurricane Andrew, the worst natural disaster in the history of the United States up to that point, slammed into

Florida and Louisiana, costing fifty-two lives and $20 billion in damages.[146] In 1992, seven of the most powerful earthquakes in the world were centered in California.[147] The mountains were literally shaking.

That same year, there were terrible tornadoes in America's heartland. Record breaking forest fires swept through California, devastating thousands of acres. Still, after 1992, there was no return to God.

In March 1993, a massive storm, known also as "the storm of the century," set records for low pressures, spawned tornadoes in Florida, produced record temperatures, and crippled the Southern United States, dumping one and a half feet of snow on Birmingham, Alabama. Three hundred deaths and $6 billion in damage were attributed to the storm.

The great flood of 1993 devastated large portions of the Mississippi and Missouri Valleys. Ten thousand homes were destroyed with fifteen million acres of agricultural land flooded. Fifty people died and fifteen billion dollars in damage was done as a result of the flood.

In July, the flooding along the Mississippi River caused 534 counties in nine states to be declared federal disaster areas with 168,340 people registered for federal assistance.[148] From 1990 through 1993, losses in our nation as a result of natural disasters surpassed those during the previous decade,[149] and yet we refused to return to God.

In January of 1994, the North Ridge, California earthquake surpassed hurricane Andrew as the costliest disaster in United States history. The 6.7 magnitude earthquake killed more than seventy people, injured nine thousand, and caused more than $20 billion in damage.[150] We also saw, in 1994, the coldest temperatures ever recorded in the Midwest and Northeast, with wind chills of 90 degrees below zero in some states.

On Palm Sunday, March 24, 1994, tornadoes left a path of destruction from North Central Alabama to the Carolinas, killing 42 people, injuring 320, and causing $107 million in damage. Twenty people died and ninety were injured in the Goshen United Methodist Church in Cherokee County, Alabama when a tornado collapsed the roof on the congregation during the Palm Sunday service.[151]

Natural disasters continued to increase.

In one week of July 1995, seven-hundred-thirty-nine residents of Chicago died in a catastrophic heat wave, making this disaster one of "the greatest and least known American disasters in modern history."[152] The 1995 heat wave surpassed both Hurricane Andrew of 1992 and the 1994 Northridge, California earthquake in

129

fatalities, killing ten and twenty times the number of people taken by these previous disasters.[153] Hurricanes Opal and Marilyn, in October and September 1995 respectively, combined for $5.1 billion in damages and forty deaths.[154]

Natural disasters continued to increase in intensity throughout the 1990s. January 1996 was marked by a blizzard, followed by severe flooding in Appalachia, the Mid-Atlantic, and the Northeast portions of our nation. February 1996 brought severe flooding to the Pacific Northwest, while the Southern Plains continued to suffer from one of the most severe droughts in their history. In September 1996, Hurricane Fran struck the coasts of North Carolina and Virginia. In all, these disasters accounted for a total loss of 233 lives and $14 billion in damages.[155]

The giant El Niño weather patterns of 1997 and 1998 unleashed everything from severe tornadoes to floods. In eight months, it caused twenty-one hundred deaths and $33 billion in damages worldwide. El Niño reached its peak in December 1997, only to be replaced by La Niña.

According to *National Geographic*, this El Niño was the deadliest in the past two centuries. Of the ten most powerful El Niños ever recorded, the four strongest have occurred since 1980.[156]

The National Climatic Data Center of the US Department of Commerce reported flooding disasters related to El Niño in 1997 and 1998 in California, Washington, Oregon, Idaho, Nevada, Montana, Arkansas, Missouri, Mississippi, Tennessee, Illinois, Kentucky, Ohio, West Virginia, North Dakota, South Dakota, Minnesota, portions of Texas, Louisiana, Alabama, Georgia, Florida, South Carolina, North Carolina, Virginia, and accounting for 278 deaths and $11.2 billion in damages.[157] El Niño was also the contributing factor in severe ice storms in the Northeast in January 1998 and in California in December 1998, along with Hurricanes Bonnie and George in August and September 1998. These created another thirty-five fatalities and $10.8 billion in damages.

However, the summer of 1998 brought severe drought to those portions of Texas and the Southeastern United States unaffected by the floods, leaving at least two hundred dead and $9 billion in damage, making the total loss for 1997 and 1998, three hundred thirteen killed and $31 billion in property loss.[158]

The decade of the 1990s ended with tornadoes in Oklahoma, Kansas, Arkansas, and Tennessee. Hurricane Floyd made landfall in eastern North Carolina in September 1999, but the worst disaster occurred in the drought which

131

gripped the eastern US and was responsible for an estimated 502 deaths.[159]

Natural disasters in 1999 caused 651 deaths and did almost $10 billion in damages.[160]

Our nation obstinately refused to return to God.

In spite of these dramatic disasters and their overwhelming impact, our nation obstinately refused to return to God, and we marched defiantly into the first decade of the new millennium.

Each decade since the 1980s saw property damage from natural disasters double or even triple, according to government figures.[161] Prior to 1987, the United States had never experienced a natural disaster with insured losses greater than $1 billion. During the first decade of 2000, multi-billion dollar natural disasters, with a corresponding increase in the loss of human life, became a regular occurence.[162]

The increasing frequency of natural disasters was evidenced by the dramatic rise in the average number of earthquakes per year as our nation moved into the new millennium. In the 1990s, there were, on average, 2869 earthquakes per year in the U.S., while the first decade of 2000 averaged 4,512 earthquakes a year.[163]

A similar increase in the number of tornadoes gave further indication that our nation had moved into the third step of exposure. In the decade of the 1990s, there was an average of 111 tornadoes per year in our nation, with thirty-six tornado related fatalities on average, each year.[164] The number of tornadoes jumped to an average of 301 each year in the first decade of 2000, and on average, forty-seven deaths per year were caused by tornadoes. However, the greatest increase in the number of tornadoes took place in the first six months of 2011, marking not only the beginning of a new decade, but also the highest frequency of tornadoes in the history of our nation. The first half of 2011 saw 730 tornadoes, and a corresponding 565 deaths caused by the tornadoes.[165] The evidence was irrefutable; we were living in a nation exposed, yet we still refused to return to God.

While tornadoes and earthquakes increased in the first decade of 2000, hurricanes and wildfires became the disasters which defined the years of 2000 through 2010. From 2000 through 2003, the drought gripping the southeastern and southwestern United States, and the wildfires resulting from the severe drought, caused $20.8 billion in damage and cost 169 lives. As the drought deepened, an additional $24 billion in damages was caused and 66 more lives were lost through 2010.[166] Twenty of those who lost their lives in 2006 were firefighters.[167]

Hurricanes, however, were the defining natural disaster of 2000 through 2010. The year 2005 was the most active hurricane season ever recorded in the United States. This was also the single worst year to date in our nation, regarding natural disasters, with the worst natural disaster ever recorded in the United States, Hurricane Katrina, occurring in August of 2005.[168]

How could we, as a nation, miss the accelerating frequency and intensity of the natural disasters which we were facing, as we experienced one hurricane after another during this decade? Hurricanes that resulted in more than $1 billion in damages during this decade are as follows:[169]

Hurricane	Year	Property Damage	Deaths
Allison (tropical storm)	2001	$5 billion	43
Isabel	2003	$5 billion	55
Charley	2004	$15 billion	35
Frances	2004	$9 billion	48
Ivan	2004	$15.4 billion	57
Jeanne	2004	$7.7 billion	28
Dennis	2005	$2 billion	15
Katrina	2005	$133.8 billion	1,833
Rita	2005	$16 billion	119
Wilma	2005	$17.1 billion	35
Dolly	2008	$1.2 billion	3
Gustav	2008	$5 billion	43
Ike	2008	$27 billion	112
Total		*$259.2 billion*	*2,426*

In spite of this explosion of hurricanes, we did not return to God. Additional damage occurred this decade as a result of severe weather episodes, storms, tornadoes, floods, and hail, much of which was spawned by these hurricanes. An additional $41 billion in property damage and 308 deaths occurred as a result of these weather events.[170]

While there were no mega-disasters to capture the nation's attention in 2007, there were still numerous localized disasters across the United States with sixty-three major federal disaster declarations issued nationwide, making 2007 one of the most active years, regarding natural disasters in our nation's history.[171] Torsten Jeworrek, board member of the German based reinsuring company, Munich Re, stated: "all the facts indicate that losses caused by weather-related natural catastrophes will continue to rise...we should not be misled by the absence of mega catastrophes in 2007."[172] The first decade of 2000 was the most active decade in our nation for national disasters, but nothing prepared us for what happened as a new decade began.

In the spring of 2011, there were major tornado outbreaks across the United States. From April 14 through 16, forty-three people were killed in one series of tornadoes,[173] and more than three hundred fifty people died in a tornado outbreak from April 25 through 28, the deadliest U.S. tornado outbreak in seventy-five years.[174][175]

Those states experiencing the greatest devastation were: Oklahoma, Arkansas, Mississippi, Tennessee, Georgia, North Carolina, Virginia, and Alabama. In Alabama alone, the tornadoes produced over 250 fatalities and $10 billion in damage, making the Alabama tornado outbreak the costliest in U.S. history.[176]

On May 22, an EF5 tornado struck Joplin, Missouri, killing at least 132 people while injuring over one thousand persons and causing approximately $3 billion in damage, making it the deadliest single U.S. tornado in sixty-four years, and the costliest single tornado of all time.[177][178]

While the increase in natural disasters in the United States has been obvious, most meteorologists choose to attribute the increase in weather related natural disasters to climatic change as a result of global warming,[179] and most seismologists attribute the increase in earthquakes to improved reporting equipment and techniques.[180]

I do not believe that the dramatic rise in frequency of earthquakes from the 1990s to the first decade of 2000 can be attributed to better equipment. With a bachelor's degree in Geology, I feel somewhat qualified to assert that there has not been enough change in either seismic equipment or reporting stations to account for the increase in the average number of earthquakes from the 1990s to the first ten years of 2000.

While I do not claim to be an expert in weather related disasters, I believe that we are experiencing increases in these natural disasters because we are a nation exposed, not as a result of global warming. It is my contention that God moved our nation into the third step of exposure in 1985 when He released natural disasters against our nation that have continued to increase significantly.

> *God has been trying to get our attention.*

In 1988, God intensified the exposure of the United States, initiating an ever expanding exposure of the sins of "His people." God is serious about our nation returning to Him. He has been trying to get our attention, and we are not listening. God has unleashed natural disasters against this nation. He has exposed the sin in the very lives of those people who are supposed to lead the nation back to Him.

What happens when these natural disasters are released and God's people refuse to lead in the return to God? God intensifies this third step of exposure by taking yet another action.

Action 3
God Exposes the Nation to Foreign Attack

Isaiah shows us the third action God takes against the exposed nation. He tells us, in verse 26, how God intensifies the exposure of a nation whose people refuse to return to Him.

Isaiah 5

26. He lifts up a banner for the distant nations, he whistles for those at the ends of the earth. Here they come, swiftly and speedily!

If exposing the sins of His people and releasing natural disasters against a nation do not cause a nation to return to Him, then God will raise up other nations to oppose the exposed nation, even attack it. He will "whistle" for the other nations to come against the exposed nation. When the exposure reaches this stage, the nation being exposed is beginning to unravel.

It happened to Israel, and later to Judah when God allowed them to be taken into captivity by Assyria and Babylon. I believe it happened to America on September 11, 2001. For the first time in the history of our nation, the mainland of the United States of America was directly attacked by a foreign power.

No longer can we sing "Thine alabaster cities gleam undimmed by human tears" without realizing that many tears were shed on that day and subsequent days, as the families of the innocent victims who died in New York, Washington, D.C., and Pennsylvania tried to piece their lives back together again.

What really happened on September 11, 2001? We witnessed the intensifying of God's exposure of America. I do not mean to imply that the victims who died on that day in any way were being singled out by God. Nothing could be further from the truth. America is being singled out by God, which means that as long as our nation refuses to return to God, there will be tragic results and innocent victims.

On September 11, 2001, we witnessed the beginning of the unraveling of our nation in more dramatic terms than we have witnessed to date. It is not that God desired for the World Trade Center Towers to collapse, the Pentagon to be attacked, or the United Airlines flight to crash in Pennsylvania, but rather, that God removed His hedge of protection from our nation because of our obstinate refusal to return to Him.

God wanted America to come back to Him long before we reached this fatal step of exposure, but America refused. God repeatedly warned us, but we rejected Him and His protection.

So now, with God's hedge of protection removed from America, we are exposed to those who would seek our destruction. Our enemies are being permitted to move against us. It is still God's desire that we would return to Him so that He could heal our land.

> *We are exposed to those who would seek our destruction.*

I believe God removed His protection from America with a broken heart, but He could not allow us to remain in open rebellion and continue to prosper. America will face its own captivity of exposure unless we humble ourselves and ask God to forgive and deliver us. We did not heed God's warnings in the exposure of the sins of those charged with the responsibility of handling His Word. We refused to correlate the natural disasters pummeling our nation with the removal of God's protection.

We did not come to God as a nation, so now other nations have been enlisted to oppose us and even overtake us. That is the horror that was unleashed on the U.S. on September 11, 2001. At 8:46 A.M. American Airlines Flight 11 crashed into the World Trade Center's North

Tower,[181] followed by United Airlines Flight 175, which hit the South Tower at 9:03 A.M.[182] Both flights had been hijacked by Islamic extremists.

Another group of hijackers flew American Airlines Flight 77 into the Pentagon at 9:37 A.M.,[183] and a fourth airplane, United Airlines Flight 93, crashed near Shanksville, Pennsylvania at 10:03 A.M., after its passengers overwhelmed the hijackers. The ultimate target was thought to be either the U.S. Capitol building or the White House.[184]

As a result of these attacks, there were a total of 2,996 deaths, including the nineteen hijackers and 2,977 victims.[185] The FBI investigation into the attacks, code-named operation PENTTBOM, was the largest and most involved investigation in the history of the FBI, encompassing more than seven thousand special agents.[186]

It was determined by this investigation that al-Qaeda, an Islamic extremist group headed by Osama bin Laden, bore responsibility for the attacks. The FBI stated that "evidence linking al-Qaeda and bin Laden to the attacks of September 11 is clear and irrefutable."[187] The Government of Great Britain reached the same conclusion regarding al-Qaeda and Osama bin Laden's responsibility for the September 11 attacks.[188]

We had become an exposed nation under attack from a foreign power. In a 1998 fatwa, or religious decree, issued by al-Qaeda, the leaders of al-Qaeda stated:

> ... in compliance with Allah's order, we issue the following fatwa to all Muslims: The ruling to kill the Americans and their allies, both civilians and military, is an individual duty for every Muslim....[189]

America was a nation at war. It was the next step in God allowing us, as a nation, to walk the path we had chosen, a path that abandoned God and His will for us, a path of exposure. Since we have chosen to walk away from God, He has released us to go the way we have selected.

Isaiah tells us that other nations will come prepared for battle against the nation that is exposed. Scripture gives a vivid description of those who will rise up against the exposed nation.

Isaiah 5

27. Not one of them grows tired or stumbles, not one slumbers or sleeps;

not a belt is loosened at the waist, not a sandal thong is broken.

28. Their arrows are sharp, all their bows are strung; their horses' hoofs seem like flint, their chariot wheels like a whirlwind.

29. Their roar is like that of the lion, they roar like young lions; they growl as they seize their prey and carry it off with no one to rescue.

30. In that day they will roar over it like the roaring of the sea. And if one looks at the land, he will see darkness and distress; even the light will be darkened by the clouds.

America is facing an enemy in the Islamic extremists unlike any enemy we have ever faced. These extremists are not limited by the borders of a single country. Their hatred for America runs deeper than simple animosity. They hate us to the very core of their being primarily because of our affiliation with Israel, one of the nations who experienced exposure because of its refusal to return to God.

The Muslim world has been experiencing economic stagnation for centuries. Most Muslim countries are not knowledge-based economies, in other words, not based on research, development, manufacturing, or industry. In 2011, President Obama stated that, apart from crude oil, the exports of the entire Middle East with its population of 400 million roughly equaled that of Switzerland.[190]

Throughout the region, young people, brimming with ideas, have been unable to fulfill their potential because of the domination of the repressive Islamic extremists. The Arab Spring, a revolutionary wave of demonstrations and protests that have been taking place in the Arab world since December 2010, was fueled, many believe, by the large percentage of educated but dissatisfied youth within the populations of these countries.[191]

While some draw hope that animosity toward the United States will decrease as a result of the revolutions sweeping the region, others see ominous signs of even greater anger focused on the United States because of these changes. Ben Stein, contributor to CBS News, stated:

> There is a gigantic regional coup by Iran taking place. We are doing very little, if anything, to stop it. We are going to regret helping the Egyptians kick out Mubarak as much as we regret helping Khomeini force out the Shah. You can call it "Arab Spring" if you want. But, with Iran now the

regional super-power, it is a lot more like an extremely bleak Mideast winter.[192]

Regardless of one's opinion about the Arab Spring, the consensus appears to have emerged that this revolt is primarily fueled by the young people who have been much abused and used by the Islamic extremists of the region. Daniel Byman, Middle Eastern expert with the Brookings Institute, and Christine Fair, an assistant professor of Peace and Security Studies at Georgetown University, say that many of the Islamic terrorists are decidedly uneducated, perhaps even untrainable individuals, who engage in the very behavior they condemn in others, as evidenced by the fact that pornography is one of the most common contents on laptops taken from the extremists.[193]

Intelligence retrieved by Predator drones and other battlefield cameras demonstrate the hypocrisy of the Islamic extremists who claim moral superiority to the Americans they so vehemently despise. Videos captured by these drones and other sources have recorded these extremists sexually gratifying themselves with each other and a wide assortment of barnyard animals, including cows and donkeys.[194]

According to ex-terrorist Abu Bacir El Assimi this same sexual perversion is aimed at the young people who are recruited by the extremists as suicide bombers.[195] The repeated rapes of these young recruits, who are between the ages of sixteen and nineteen, become a primary motivation for these young people to engage in suicide bombings. They would rather die than continue living in the abuse.[196]

Is it any wonder that the pent up anger and frustration coming from those who "roar like young lions" (v. 29) is aimed at the only acceptable object of hatred in their culture–America? These young Muslims are trained not only to hate Americans, but to sacrifice their lives to alleviate their pain and carry out their hatred. They are not bound by national loyalty, but have been led to believe that the source of all their problems is America, and we have become a nation exposed to their hatred.

The War on Terror, which began with the attacks on the World Trade Center on September 11, 2001, has become the longest lasting war in the history of our nation, costing our nation eighty-eight hundred deaths, and forty-six thousand Americans wounded or injured.[197]

A March 2011 Congressional Research Service report states that the price tag through fiscal year 2011, for the War on Terror, will be $1.283 trillion, including military operations, base security, reconstruction, foreign aid, embassy costs, and veteran's health care.[198] With our nation now engaged in fighting the global War on Terror on numerous fronts, there seems to be no relief in sight.

The execution of Osama bin Laden on May 2, 2011[199] may be an important milestone for our nation in the War on Terror, but it does not radically alter the challenging situation facing America.[200] There are active terrorist cells operating in Yemen, Somalia, North Africa, Iraq, and Europe. The Taliban, operating out of Afghanistan and Pakistan, are entirely autonomous and have derived no leadership support from al-Qaeda. The death of Osama bin Laden will have negligible effect on the Taliban.[201] Osama bin Laden is dead. His organization, its offshoots, and the War on Terror are all very much alive.[202]

As Isaiah states, the enemies of an exposed nation, which have been summoned by God, will not "slumber or sleep." (v. 27) They will attack the nation with sharp arrows (v. 29) and "bows strung." (v. 29) They will stand ready to use whatever weapon is at their disposal to seek the destruction of the exposed nation.

We have seen suicide bombings and attempted bombings using everything from shoes to baby bottles to underwear, all in an attempt to kill as many Americans as possible. Many citizens of the Middle East see this as entirely acceptable.

A 2004 Pew Research Survey found that suicide bombings against Americans were seen as justifiable by Jordanians (70 percent), Pakistanis (46 percent), and Turks (31 percent.)[203] However, the obsession to obtain weapons of mass destruction to use against the United States is a driving force behind many terrorist groups. Charles Curtis, president and chief operating officer of the Nuclear Threat Initiative, has stated:

> The security threat posed by nuclear weapons is not a new or unanalyzed danger. What is new is the emergence of a particularly virulent form of 'sacred terrorism' operating on a global scale with substantial resources and with a demonstrated willingness to kill on a grand scale.[204]

Curtis continued:

> ...technological advances and the operations of a global economy may soon outpace our defenses.... The enemy that we face does not have borders to defend, people to protect, or territory to control.... Collateral damage is not in their vocabulary.... The threat comes from those who hijack the Islamic faith to demonize the

West; declare the United States and its allies enemies of Islam; blame them for the ills that befall Muslim nations; spread this view to as many Muslims as possible; and incite violence against America, its people, its property, and its allies.[205]

The Islamic extremists are determined to destroy America, and that could very well happen unless we return to God and His protection. Isaiah states:

Isaiah 5

30b. and if one looks at the land, he will see darkness and distress: even the light will be darkened by the clouds.

Could this refer to the clouds of a nuclear weapon unleashed against a modern day exposed nation? It is my fervent prayer that we return to God before we reach the point of finding out. As Charles Curtis further stated regarding the enemy our nation faces:

In the long run, WMDs (weapons of mass destruction), particularly chemical and biological weapons, are going to become easier to make, not harder; so the urge to use them must become less, not more. We can no longer protect ourselves solely by the strength of our arms and the strength of our alliances or even with new partnerships with old adversaries. We have to learn how to diminish hatred.[206]

I believe that Charles Curtis has accurately stated the dilemma facing our nation. I also believe, however, that it is beyond the capacity of the United States to address the hatred directed toward it by the Islamic extremists until our people return to God. We will continue living exposed to the hatred of those who have been summoned by God to oppose us unless we return to Him and the Christian principles which gave birth to our nation.

These enemies have attacked us because we have removed ourselves from God's protection. The Islamic extremists hate us because we are Americans. They could very well be the ones who destroy America, if we refuse to return to God. Our military might is not enough to insure our survival.

If Iran does emerge as the regional superpower in the Middle East, as some have predicted is likely following the Arab Spring Revolutions,[207] and if it persists with enriching uranium for possible weapons use,[208] the very people who hate America could possibly acquire the nuclear weapons of mass destruction they have been passionately seeking.

On February 9, 2010, Iran announced that it had produced enriched uranium,[209] and two days later, the Iranian president, Mahmoud Ahmadinejad, announced that Iran was now a nuclear state.[210] Ali Akbar Salehi, head of the Atomic Energy Organization of Iran, told Reuters, on the same day as President Ahmadinejad's announcement, that their 20 percent enrichment production was going very well, adding, "we can enrich up to 100 percent" (the amount required to produce a nuclear weapon).[211] We must return to God before it is too late. Thus far, however, America has refused to heed the evidence that we are an exposed nation.

The third step of exposure, which God allows a nation to experience when it refuses to return to Him, is the step of superlatives. In this third step, God uncovers the sins of His own people in unprecedented numbers. He further releases the deadliest and most costly natural disasters the nation has ever experienced.

If neither of these actions causes the exposed nation to return to Him, God will allow the nation to be attacked by a foreign power. I am convinced that the pattern of return and renewal by which God interacts with the nations had remained consistent in America's history until fairly recently. The pattern, simply stated, involved:

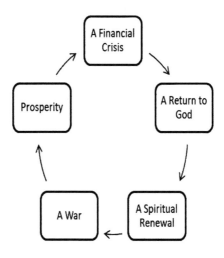

For America, this pattern began to break down in the 1920s as we embraced the ideas of Karl Marx, Charles Darwin, Sigmund Freud, and Friedrich Nietzsche. As these ideas began to permeate our classrooms, eventually emerging as the dominate philosophies in our educational system, the pattern of returning to God and spiritual renewal in America began to break down.

We were drifting, as a nation, away from God, and it became obvious that we were removing ourselves from God's protection and becoming an exposed nation. As our nation worked its way through each step of exposure, our departure from God continued to deepen, and our resolve not to return to God became even stronger. Thus far, America has continued its march away from God through the first three steps of exposure.

First Step of Exposure (Isaiah 5:1-4)
1950s

Following the hardship of the depression in the 1930s and the bloodshed of World War II in the 1940s, America did not return to God and subsequently moved into its first step of exposure. In this step, God reminded America of the many benefits it had experienced because of its relationship with Him. Our refusal to return to God and express gratitude for our blessings was marked by a dramatic increase in violence in our nation, in keeping with our deepening departure from God. As a result of our refusal to return to God at this point, America moved into the second step of exposure.

Second Step of Exposure (Isaiah 5:5-23)
1962

Our nation responded to the favor God had shown us and His reminding us of His kindness in the 1950s by openly defying Him. On June 25, 1962, in the Supreme Court ruling *En-*

gel v. Vitale, the students in our public schools were denied the opportunity of praying openly to God in school to seek His blessing on the students, their parents, their teachers, and their country.[212] It is my contention that, at that point, God, with a broken heart, allowed us to remove ourselves from His Protection as we arrogantly continued withdrawing our nation from Him.

Our movement into this second step of exposure became evident almost immediately with a dramatic increase in violent crime and an equally dramatic decline in productivity. We were in an ever deepening departure from God. The ideas and concepts which we embraced, as a nation, in the 1920s had become an increasing part of our national thought process, further solidifying our withdrawal from God and our refusal to return to Him.

Our deepening exposure became evident almost immediately as we witnessed a radical change in our national life, which was now characterized by greed (vv. 8-10), escapism (vv. 11-17), arrogance toward God (vv.18-19), a confusion of good and evil (v. 20), truth replaced by personal opinion (v. 21), and political corruption (vv. 22-23).

We had become a nation exposed, and because we refused to return to God, we moved into the third step of exposure, where God took specific actions to get our national attention.

Third Step of Exposure (Isaiah 5:24-30)
1985

America moved into the third step of exposure as God took three actions to get our attention and call us to return to Him:

Action 1
God Exposes His Own People (v. 25a)
1988

With the collapse of Jim Bakker and Jimmy Swaggert, and their ministries, in 1988, the floodgates were opened in America regarding the exposure of those who have identified themselves as God's people. This exposure continued to gain momentum as the distance between God and our nation widened.

Action 2
God Releases Natural Disasters (v. 25b)
1985

The exposure of the sins of God's people and the release of natural disasters of growing magnitude occur practically simultaneously. As the frequency and intensity of natural disasters continued to increase in the exposed nation, God continued to extend His offer of protection. If America would return to God, it could experience, once again, His presence and protection.

In 1985, God released a series of natural disasters on America that have been increasing with each decade. Yet, we have refused to see the signs unfolding around us, and we have refused to return to God, so God intensified the third step of exposure by taking a third action.

Action 3
God Exposes the Nation to Foreign Attack
(vv. 26-30)
 2001

On September 11, 2001, for the first time in our history, the United States was attacked by a foreign power on our own soil. Our enemies, Islamic extremists, are bent on our destruction and are committed to insuring that America is subjugated to the Muslim agenda. Our military strength is no match for their hatred.

Our only hope is to return to God. Our nation has exhibited no evidence of ending our withdrawal from God. The exposure has increased as we continue to move toward the final and fatal fourth step of exposure.

Chapter Five

The Fourth Step of Exposure: Restoration or Destruction

America has continued its withdrawal from God and appears determined to continue on that path, regardless of the consequences. On June 19, 2011, NBC Sports was broadcasting the US Open Golf Tournament. One segment of the program showed small children with hands over their hearts reciting the pledge of allegiance to the flag of the United States of America.

Suddenly, the scene shifted to a soldier saluting the flag, interrupting the student's pledge. The scene, just as suddenly, returned to the students as they resumed their pledge, but not at the point where they had been interrupted. The video of the student's pledge had been edited, and one phrase had been omitted from their otherwise flawless pledge. The phrase that had been omitted was, *under God.*

NBC apologized profusely for what they stated was an unintended mistake. This mistake, however, indicates a great deal about America. We are a nation that has withdrawn itself from God's protection. We are, therefore, a nation exposed. In all honesty, we cannot claim to be "one nation under God" if we face what we have become and just how exposed we are.

We have seen the first three steps of exposure that God releases a nation to experience when it refuses to return to Him.

Step 1
God Reveals the Nation's Prosperity.
I believe this happened in the post-World War II economic boom of the 1950s.

Step 2
God Removes the Nation's Protection.
It is my contention that this happened in1962, with the Supreme Court decision, *Engel v. Vitale,* which restricted school prayer.

Step 3
God Releases the Nation's Punishment.
I am convinced that we moved into this third step of exposure in 1985 with the increase in natural disasters we began experiencing as a nation.

This step deepened in 1988 with the exposure of the wrongs being done in the Jim Bakker and Jimmy Swaggert Ministries, along with the flood of exposures that have occurred regarding other ministries. When we still refused to return to God, He increased His response to our rebellion by inviting other nations to attack us. That is exactly what happened on September 11, 2001. We still refused to return to God.

Unless we return to God, He will whistle for other nations to come for us, roaring like lions. They will carry us away and there will be no one to rescue us.

Our nation is not only being attacked from enemies without, it is deteriorating within. Nearly every social institution in America is in chaos. Situational ethics and moral relativism are pervading every facet of public life. Our economy is in shambles. We are a debtor nation.

Any attempt to call us back to the truth of Scripture invokes cries of, "Don't impose your morality on me!" We are in a moral free-fall. We can no longer afford to ignore the exposure that we are experiencing. A few spiritual leaders in America recognized what was happening to our nation over a decade ago, but we did not heed their warning.

Jack Hayford

There is not a believer in this nation with any...discernment or sensitivity in their spirit who does not understand that we are in a time of crisis.[213]

Chuck Colson

You smell the decay, you smell the rotting flesh of Western civilization today...[214]

D. James Kennedy

[People believe that] there is no God that is going to sit in judgment upon the actions of men.... It is astounding to me that people cannot see that, having forgotten God, we are indeed in the process of destroying ourselves.[215]

Dr. Charles Stanley

Unless there is a revival, this nation is going to get worse and worse.[216]

Dr. John Hagee

...It's over unless there is a broad, sweeping revival of repentance.[217]

As a people, we refused to heed the warnings of those among us who saw what was happening. We just went about our lives

Since our exposure is real, who will lead us back to God? There is only one group of people who have what is necessary to stem the tide of exposure and return us to God—the people of God. Our nation's fate depends on the people of God humbling themselves, praying, seeking His face, and turning from their wicked ways. God's Word states it clearly:

2 Chronicles 7

14. "if my people, who are called by my name, will humble themselves and pray and seek my face and turn from their wicked ways, then will I hear from heaven and will forgive their sin and will heal their land."

God promises to hear the cries of His people, to forgive the sins of His people, and to heal the exposed land in which they live. If at least a remnant of God's people will "humble themselves and pray and seek [His] face and turn from their wicked ways," then the march away from God can be halted, a return to God can begin, and the exposure of our nation can end; then God will heal our nation.

161

Yet, no remnant of God's people is rising up to accept this challenge and the responsibility to humbly lead our nation back to God. God's people are too busy blaming others for the exposure of America to honestly humble themselves.

Many have convinced themselves that, if we can just elect the right political officials, we can initiate a return to God. While I am certainly in favor of electing politicians who believe and live out the Christian principles which had previously caused our nation to live consistently in the pattern of returning to God and experiencing spiritual renewal, I know that our hope does not lie in the political arena. Our hope is spiritual, not political.

In the fourth step of exposure, God calls out a group of people to warn the nation in rebellion to turn back to Him before He destroys the exposed nation. If we do not heed the warning of the remnant, we will be destroyed. There is no "next step" of exposure. It is return to God now or face continued deterioration, and ultimately destruction. This is America's last opportunity to survive.

Who is God looking for in the remnant of people that He wants to use? They are the people who will say, "No matter what happens to America, we will not abandon our God and His mandate to rise up and make a difference."

162

There are six actions that you and I must take to be counted among the remnant of people who stay close to God, and who God can use in an exposed nation.

Action One
You Must Know God (vv.1-4)

Isaiah was living in an exposed nation. The people of God had divided into two kingdoms: Israel, the Northern Kingdom; and Judah, the Southern Kingdom. This division occurred in 931 B.C. following the reign of Solomon. While Isaiah was primarily a prophet to the Southern Kingdom of Judah from approximately 739 to 681 B.C., he was also watching events unfold in the Northern Kingdom of Israel, a nation rapidly progressing through the steps of exposure.

Isaiah addressed, in Chapter 5, the events unfolding in Israel as he revealed the various stages of exposure that a nation goes through when it refuses to return to God. Using the example of a vineyard that had its hedge of protection removed, and ultimately fell into disarray, Isaiah asserted, "The vineyard of the Lord Almighty is the house [nation] of Israel..." (Isaiah 5:7).

Isaiah pleaded with the people of Judah to heed the events unfolding in Israel. (See Isaiah 5:3) Eventually, during the ministry of Isaiah, the nation of Israel was taken captive in 722 B.C. by the Assyrians, and its people were uprooted and resettled into other nations. Israel had progressed rapidly through all four stages of exposure to finally cease to exist as a nation, because right up to the end of its existence, Israel refused to return to God.

Isaiah did not want to see the same thing happen to Judah. He could see that they were already a nation pulling away from God and His protection. Isaiah's ministry was one of calling Judah to return to God. Unfortunately, Judah did not heed Isaiah's warning. In a little over one hundred years following the ministry of Isaiah, in 586 B.C., Judah ceased to exist as a nation, having been taken captive by Babylon.

The same fate of destruction awaits America, if we do not return to God. I am convinced that we are standing on the cusp of the fourth step of exposure. If we step into it by refusing to return to God, we too will cease to exist. After Isaiah had shared his heartbreaking message regarding the steps of exposure a nation in rebellion against God must go through, he found himself standing outside the temple of God.

Isaiah 6

1. In the Year that King Uzziah died, I saw the Lord seated on a throne, high and exalted, and the train of His robe filled the temple.

King Uzziah's death, about 758 B.C., was the setting for Isaiah's visit to the temple. Uzziah had died as the result of a judgment from God. The king thought that he could perform the duties of a priest, even though he had not been called to be a priest. He acted with such arrogance and pride, that he exposed himself to the discipline of God and was struck with leprosy.

It was during this dark period in Israel's history that Isaiah went to the temple and wrote, "I saw the Lord...." God was making His presence known to Isaiah, even as Isaiah was watching the impending destruction of Israel, and Judah beginning to follow the same path of exposure. God is still making His presence known to us in spite of what is happening in America today.

Isaiah saw "...the Lord seated on a throne, high and exalted, and the train of His robe filled the temple" (v. 1). Isaiah was reminded that no matter what events were unfolding around him, God was still on His throne. God was still in control. It is important for us to remember that our hope does not rest in America. Our hope rests in "the Lord seated on a throne." He is "high and exalted." He is not controlled by or subject to our whims or our choices. He is Almighty God, and He is greater than any situation we would ever face. He is in control. Isaiah continued:

Isaiah 6

> *2. Above him were seraphs, each with six wings: With two wings they covered their faces, with two they covered their feet, and with two they were flying.*
> *3. And they were calling to one another: "Holy, holy, holy is the Lord Almighty: The whole earth is full of his glory."*
> *4. At the sound of their voices the doorposts and thresholds shook and the temple was filled with smoke.*

Verses 2-3 describe the seraphs—angels who guard the holiness of God—celebrating His holiness in worship. Verse 4 tells us that the smoke from the consuming fire who is our God filled the house.

Our nation must understand that you don't toy with God's guidelines and not get burned. That is why God wants people who know Him intimately and are willing to listen to His voice.

The only way a person can be in contact with God is by establishing a personal relationship with His Son, Jesus. In fact, Jesus said, "I am the way and the truth and the life. No one comes to the Father except through me." [218] In many ways, this is the most politically incorrect statement that anyone could ever make. The politically correct viewpoint in our nation today is to say that there are many ways to approach God, but that is not the truth. The Bible tells us, when speaking of Jesus:

Acts 4

12. Salvation is found in no one else, for there is no other name under heaven given to men by which we must be saved. [219]

Jesus is our only hope of salvation. Apart from Him we have no hope. If you have never established a personal relationship with Jesus, then you will be exposed with the nation that is exposed, and you will spend eternity separated

> *There were many Christians who died on September 11, 2001.*

from God, suffering the consequences of that exposure.

Does that mean that those people who have a relationship with Jesus are immune from the consequences that God unleashes on an exposed nation? No! In fact, there were many Christians who died on September 11, 2001, when our nation was attacked.

They were not, however, simply victims of the terrorist's attack. They were released to join their God in the home He had prepared for them in heaven. Those who died on September 11, as on any day, who did not know God, will be forever separated from God, because they did not come to know Him through His Son, Jesus.

Your only hope of surviving the exposure is to commit your life to Jesus Christ by admitting that you are a sinner and surrendering control of your life to Jesus. Only then are you protected for eternity, and only then are you assured of an eternity lived in the presence of God.

There are those who insist that it is too narrow to say there is only one way to God. If you were in a burning house, and a fire fighter fought his way through the flames to show you the one way out, would you refuse to go, because having only one way out was too narrow?

If you were dying of a disease, and a physician offered you the only cure available for the disease, would you refuse the cure, because only having one cure for your disease is too narrow, or because the cure was only available as a shot and you prefer it in pill form?

God has, through His Son, Jesus, provided us with the only hope we have for knowing Him. It would be even more foolish to refuse God's offer of our only hope of knowing Him, than refusing the one way out of a burning building or the one cure for an otherwise terminal disease. Waiting for God to do something more, something else, or something better, than the sacrifice of His Son on the cross is the height of arrogance. There is nothing more, nothing else, nothing better. Jesus is the only way to the Father.

As a nation progresses through the stages of exposure, the exclusivity of Jesus as the way to God becomes less and less palatable to the people of that nation. The difficulty some people have accepting Jesus as the only way to God does not change whether or not it is true. How many legs would a dog have if you called its tail a leg? It would still only have four legs. Calling a dog's tail a leg does not make it a leg.

Jesus told us plainly, "I am the Way, the Truth, and the Life. No one comes to the Father except through Me."[220] Only through Jesus can we come to know God, and knowing God is our only hope of survival in an exposed nation that refuses to return to Him.

If you have never established a personal relationship with Jesus Christ and would be willing to surrender your life to Him, then pray this prayer:

> *Dear God, I know that Jesus is Your Son, and that He died on the cross, and was raised from the dead. I know that I have sinned and need your forgiveness.*
>
> *I repent and turn from my sins and surrender control of my life to you, Jesus. I commit myself to Jesus as my Savior and Lord. Thank you for saving me. In Jesus' name I ask this. Amen.*

By committing your life to Jesus through this prayer, you are among those God can use in a nation that is exposed. However, this is not all that is required.

Action Two
You Must Be Broken (v. 5)

Once Isaiah saw God on His throne, he realized that he had entered into the presence of God. Isaiah had known God, but suddenly, Isaiah saw God and then himself as he really was.

Isaiah 6

5. "Woe to me!" I cried, "I am ruined! For I am a man of unclean lips, and my eyes have seen the King, the Lord Almighty"

When Isaiah found himself exposed to the holiness and glory of God, he said, "I am ruined." The word *ruined* in the original language of the Scripture means to disintegrate. Isaiah was saying, "I am falling to pieces because I have a dirty mouth." Isaiah was overwhelmed with his own sin and his response was to confess it to God. Isaiah had become a broken man. He realized that only God could make him whole. Isaiah also realized that he lived in a nation of broken people; people who were determined to chart their own course away from God.

America is in the condition it is in because God's people have not been willing to admit their brokenness apart from God. We cannot come into the presence of God with pride. We must come with brokenness. If you want to be counted among the remnant that God can use, you must also be broken over the sins of our nation.

For a nation to return to God, it must come back to Him with brokenness. This is the very reason many people and most, if not all, exposed nations refuse to return to God; because, to return to God, you must lay down your pride and come to Him in broken humility.

Action Three
You Must Be Clean (vv. 6-7)

Once we start the process of returning to God by coming to Him in brokenness, He will not leave us broken.

Isaiah 6

6. Then one of the seraphs flew to me with a live coal in his hand, which he had taken with tongs from the altar.

*7. With it he touched my mouth
and said, "See, this has touched
your lips; your guilt is taken
away and your sin atoned for."*

God wants to come to the broken sinner
who has tasted His presence. This coal was
brought from the altar. This was the brass altar
in the outer court of the temple that represented
death and Calvary, the place of sacrifice and re-
demption.

The angel of God brought this coal to
Isaiah. God was saying, in essence, "I know you
are broken and sinful and worthless, but I am
going to add value to your life. By the blood that
has been shed for you, I am cleansing you!"

God is not looking for perfect people;
He is looking for people who have experienced
the cleansing of His presence. You are not qualified until you are clean, and you can lose your
qualification to be used by God when you stop
allowing Him to cleanse you.

If you think you can harbor secret sin in
your heart and still let God use you to make a
difference, you are very wrong. You must be
clean before God, if you want to make a difference in your family, place of business, sphere of
influence, or even your nation. To be counted
among the remnant of people who stay in close
proximity to God in a nation that is exposed,

you must allow God to clean you up on a regular basis so He can use you.

Action Four
You Must Be Called (v. 8)

Once God has cleaned us, we are ready for Him to use us in the exposed nation.

Isaiah 6

8. Then I heard the voice of the Lord saying, "Whom shall I send? And who will go for us?" And I said, "Here am I. Send me!"

Isaiah doesn't speak with brashness, pride, or arrogance; it is with brokenness and humility that he says, "Here am I. Send me!" Who wants a broken-down prophet who has to have his mouth cleansed? God does! God wants people who have been cleansed by the blood of Jesus. You serve because God calls you, not because it is a good idea. In fact, God has a call for everyone to represent Him in some way.

Who will represent God to our exposed nation? It can only be those who have been cleansed and called by God. They will not be popular in a culture that has chosen to ignore

God. They will not be celebrated for their courage, but instead they will be attacked.

Being God's messenger in an exposed nation will demand a high price, because people living a lie resent hearing the truth. However, serving God in a nation that is exposed occurs because He calls you, not because it is easy.

Action Five
You Must be Faithful (vv. 9-12)

Many say they want to be used by God but give up. They quit because they look only at external results. They do not really understand what ministry looks like in an exposed nation.

Isaiah 6

9. He said, "Go and tell this people: 'Be ever hearing, but never understanding; be ever seeing, but never perceiving.'
10. Make the heart of this people calloused; make their ears dull and close their eyes. Otherwise they might see with their eyes, hear with their ears, understand with their hearts, and turn and be healed."

175

God told Isaiah to warn His nation even though they would not listen. God explained to Isaiah that the people were going to be insensitive to what He had to say. Few would be converted, and no one would be healed, because their hearts were already hardened. No wonder Isaiah responded with a question.

Isaiah 6

11. Then I said, "For how long, O Lord?" And he answered:
"Until the cities lie ruined and without inhabitant, until the houses are left deserted and the fields ruined and ravaged,
12. until the Lord has sent everyone far away and the land is utterly forsaken."

In other words, God was telling Isaiah that he must continue warning His nation until the exposure was complete. If no one listened, it was not the fault of the messenger, as long as the messenger was representing God.

God provides a sobering picture to Isaiah of what an exposed nation looks like once the fourth step of the exposure has been completed. It would be hard to imagine America coming to this point, but this is exactly where America will end up if it refuses to return to God. God uses words and phrases like, *ruined; without inhabitant; deserted; ravaged* (v. 11); *everyone far away; forsaken* (v. 12).

How do you measure the success of a ministry in an exposed nation that is careening toward destruction? The true criterion of success is not measured in visible results in an exposed nation. Success is measured in your faithfulness. God holds us accountable for living and telling the truth. It is our responsibility to do both until, either the nation returns to God and is restored by God, or the nation is destroyed.

Action 6
You Must Be Involved (v. 13)

God made a promise to Isaiah that is the same promise He makes to those who are His remnant in the nation exposed.

Isaiah 6

13. "And though a tenth remains in the land, it will again be laid waste. But as the terebinth and oak leave stumps when they are cut down, so the holy seed will be the stump in the land."

177

God told Isaiah that if even a tenth of the people survived the destruction of the fourth stage of exposure, they would be consumed before it was all finished. Then God went on to tell Isaiah that, while most of the nation wouldn't listen, there would be a remnant; a "holy seed" that would listen. There would still be a stump remaining that showed evidence of life.

As far as you and I are concerned regarding America, that "holy seed" becomes the whole focus and energy of our ministry and mission. You may not personally turn an entire nation around, but you can reach that remnant in your sphere of influence. You can decide how you will live your life.

The decision we are honestly facing today in America is; "Will I be part of the remnant that has chosen to stay faithful to God and involved in representing Him to a nation that is accelerating its departure from Him, or will I simply stay part of the general population heading for the destruction of the fourth step of exposure?" The choice belongs to each one of us, individually. You may not be able to turn the entire nation back to God; Isaiah couldn't, but you can make a difference.

You can witness to those with whom you live and associate. You can be faithful in your character. You can put your confidence in

God, and you *will* make a difference. That is what God is saying to us.

In December of 1991, the Soviet Union disintegrated into fifteen separate countries, as the world watched in amazement.[221] Many believe that the process for this dissolution was dramatically accelerated on May 1, 1990 when the Soviet crowds gathered at the annual May Day parade, usually reserved for a display of military might, and began to take over the celebration and impose their own agenda on the parade.[222]

One account of what occurred on that day, while it cannot be fully authenticated, has some degree of plausibility. The story goes that Mikhail Gorbachev was watching the annual May Day parade from his place of prominence in the Kremlin. As the tanks and missiles of the Soviet Army paraded by, a lone figure quietly made his way out to the middle of the parade. It happened so quickly and unexpectedly that the guards could only watch.

There was an audible gasp from the massive crowd of onlookers as this man thrust a wooden cross high into the air. He had worked his way into the very center of the Soviet Union's massive display of military power with a cross held high. With the attention of the crowd fixed on him, he shouted at the top of his lungs, "Christ is risen!"

The crowd that had been passively observing the parade became animated. They leapt to their feet and began to chant with one voice the Russian Orthodox Church response: "Christ is risen indeed! Christ is risen indeed!" Some sociologists tell us that shout could very well be the very thing that marked the death of communism.

> *That shout marked the death of communism.*

Sometimes, all it takes is one person willing to hold high the cross and say, "I will stand, Lord, regardless of what this nation does." I challenge you to be that person.

It is estimated that over 287 Christians are martyred every day in the world for the crime of loving Jesus. That is roughly twelve per hour or one every five minutes. Since the cessation of hostilities in the Sudan, the annual average number of deaths of Christians per year has declined from a high of one hundred sixty thousand in 2000 to an estimated one hundred five thousand deaths in 2011. One amazing story of commitment to Christ came from the persecution of the Sudanese Christians.[223] Dr. Bob Moorehead, in his book *Words Aptly Spoken*, recounted the following story.

A young African man was about to be martyred for his faith. No matter how brutal the torture or the threats of execution, he would not renounce his faith or stop proclaiming the gospel of Jesus Christ. Finally, he was executed for his faith. However, the night before he died, he wrote these words and left them in the room where he had been held:

> I am part of the fellowship of the unashamed. The die has been cast. I have stepped over the line. The decision has been made. I am a disciple of Christ. I won't back up, let up, slow down, back away, or be still.

> My past is redeemed. My present makes sense. My future is secure. I'm finished and done with low living, sight walking, smooth knees, colorless dreams, tamed vision, worldly talking, cheap giving, and dwarfed goals. My face is set. My gait is fast. My goal is heaven. My road is narrow. My way is rough. My companions are few. My Guide is reliable. My mission is clear.

> I won't give up, shut up, or let up until I have stayed up, stored

up, prayed up for the cause of Jesus Christ. I must go until He comes, give until I drop, preach until everyone knows, work until He stops me, and when He comes for His own, He will have no trouble recognizing me because my banner will be clear![224]

How clear is your banner? How loud is your voice? How strong is your stand? As never before, America needs your voice and your leadership.

I pray that you will commit yourself to the purpose God has for you, and I challenge you to make yourself available to be God's representative to an exposed nation.

Notes

1 Bill Bright, *Red Sky in the Morning* (Orlando, FL: New Life Publications, 1998), p. 54.

2 Isaiah Thomas, ed., *The Works of President Edwards, Vol. III* (Worchester, MA: Isaiah Thomas, 1808-1809), p. 14-19.

3 Dr. D. James Kennedy interview by John N. Damoose in Ft. Lauderdale, Florida in 1996.

4 Bill Bright, p. 67.

5 Brian H. Edwards, *Revival! A People Saturated With God* (Darlington, Co. Durham, England: Evangelical Press, 1990), p. 50.

6 Bill Bright, p. 79.

7 From President Abraham Lincoln's second inaugural address, March 4, 1865.

8 Malcolm McDow and Alvin L. Reid, *Firefall: How God Has Shaped History Through Revivals* (Nashville, TN: Broadman and Holman Publishers, 1997) p. 278.

9 Brian H. Edwards, p. 43-44.

10 ibid. p.44.

11 Friedrich Nietzsche, *The Gay Science,* s.108, translated by Walter Kaufmann.

12 Harvard Sitkoff, *Fifty Years Later: The New Deal Evaluated,* (Philadelphia: Temple University Press, 1985), p. 3, 4.

13 *Victims of the Oklahoma City Bombing.* (USA Today. Associated Press. June 20, 22001.)

14 *Timeline of Worldwide School Shootings,* (Infoplease.com; retrieved July 7, 2010)

15 Fredrich Nietzsche, *Nachlass,* translation by A. Danto.

16 *War Casualties Pass 9/11 Death Toll,* (CBS News. September 22, 2006.) Retrieved July 7, 2010

17 Andy Server, *The 00's: Goodbye (at Last) to the Decade from Hell. Time Magazine*. November 24, 2009

18 ibid

19 ibid

20 ibid

21 ibid

22 ibid

23 ibid

24 Tim Reid. *Barack Obama's 'Guns and Religion' Gives Hillary Clinton a Chance. The London Times*. 1 Virginia Street, London, E98. ixy. April 14, 2008

25 John Eidsmoe, *God and Caesar: Christian Faith and Political Action*. (Westchester, IL: Crossway Books, 1984), p. 215.

26 Christopher Columbus from his personal diary, *Book of Prophecies* in *Life and Voyages of Christopher Columbus*. Washington Irving (New York: The Cooperative Publication Society, Inc., 1892), p.41.

27 Bjorn Landstrom, *Columbus* (New York: The MacMillan Co., 1966), p.66-75.

28 George Barna, *The Index of Leading Spiritual Indicators*, (Dallas: Word Publishing, 1996), p.55.

29 ibid, p. 57.

30 Joe Arpaio, *America's Toughest Sheriff* (Arlington, TX: Summit Publishers, 1996), p. xviii.

31 Patrick Fagan and Robert Moffitt, *Issues 96: The Candidate's Briefing Book*. Washington, D.C.: The Heritage Foundation, 1996), p.2-5.

32 ibid

33 Federal Bureau of Investigations, Bureau of Justice Statistics, *FBI Uniform Crime Reports* (Washington D.C., GPO, 1997)

34 Federal Bureau of Investigation, Bureau of Justice Statistics, *Homicide Trends in the United States.* James Alan Fox. Marianne W. Zanitz, July 2010.

35 Federal Bureau of Investigation, Bureau of Justice Statistics, *Crime Victimization*, Michael Rand, September 2009.

36 Eric Johnson, *Say You Want a Revolution*, (DeBary, FL: Longwood Communication, 1994) p. 224.

37 *Aughts Were a Lost Decade for U.S. Economy, Workers.* Neil Irwin. (*The Washington Post.* January 2, 2010.)

38 ibid

39 ibid

40 *http://creditcards.com*, (Retrieved July 11, 2010)

41 ibid

42 ibid

43 *Debt Commission Chiefs Give Gloomy Fiscal Outlook,* Dan Balz. (*The Washington Post.* July 11, 2010.)

44 Jim Bakker, *I Was Wrong.* (Nashville: Thomas Nelson, 1996), p. 531-534.

45 Luke 9:25 (NIV).

46 *High Society: How Substance Abuse Ravages America and What To Do About It.* Joseph A. Califano, Jr. (Public Affairs Press. As quoted at *www.casacolumbia.org/.* The National Center on Addiction and Substance Abuse.) Retrieved on July 12, 2010.

47 *Shoveling Up II: The Impact of Substance Abuse on Federal, State, and Local Budgets.* (pdf. *www.casacolumbia.org/.* The National Center on Addiction and Substance Abuse.) Retrieved July 12, 2010.

48 *Wasting the Best and Brightest: Substance Abuse at America's Colleges and Universities.* (pdf. *www.casacolumbia.org/.* The National Center on Addiction and Substance Abuse.) Retrieved July 12, 2010.

49 David Barton, *America: To Pray or Not to Pray,* (Aledo, TX: Wallbuilders Press, 1991), p.44.

50 ibid, p.25

51 ibid

52 Edwin Mees III, Letters to the Editor: *Thinking About Crime,* (Harper's, November 1985).

53 U.S. Labor Department, Bureau of Statistics, *Productivity Trends in Manufacturing in the U.S. and 11 Other Countries,* Do'nato Alvarez and Brian Cooper. (Monthly Labor Review 107, January 1984). p.56-57.

54 McManus, Mike and Harriet. *Living Together: Myths, Risks, & Answers.* (Howard Books: Simon & Schuster, 2008).

55 ibid

56 ibid

57 ibid

58 David Burton, op.cit.p.99

59 McManus, op.cit.

60 The Psychological Bulletin (July 1998).

61 *USA Weekend* (August 21-23, 1982).

62 President Bill Clinton, *Presidential Proclamation.* (June 1999).

63 Domenico Montanaro, *Poll Shows Support for Gay Marriage.* (First Read, 2009-Apr-30, at: *http://firstread.msnbc.msn.com/*)

64 Jay McDonough. *Gay Marriage Will Be Legal by 2012.* (Swimming Freestyle Blog, at: http://www.swimming freestyle.net/

65 Frank Newport, *Six Out of Ten Americans Say Homosexual Relations Should be Recognized as Legal.* (Gallup News Service. 2003-May-15, at: *www.glapn.org/.../wnews179.htm*

66 Carl F. H. Henry, *Twilight of a Great Civilization.* (Westchester, IL: Crossway Books, 1988), p. 170.

67 George Washington (1796), *Farewell Address, The Avalon Project at Yale Law School.* (on-line, URL: *http://www.yale.edu/lawweb/avalon/washing.htm.*

68 Robert Wickes, *Frederick Nietzsche – Early Writings: 1872-1876, The Stanford Encyclopedia of Philosophy.* (Spring 2008 Edition, Edward N. Zolta (ed.))

69 Todd May, 1993, *Between Genealogy and Epistemology: Philosophy, Politics in the Thought of Michael Foucault.* (With reference to Althussen and Balibar, 1970.)

70 *Encyclopedia of Philosophy, Vol.2*, Dewey, John, with Richard J. Bernstein, p.383 (Macmillan, 1969).

71 Walter Truett Anderson, 1996. *The Fontanao Postmodernism Reader.*

72 Abraham Lincoln, at: *http://www.brainyquote.com/quote4s/quot.* Retrieved July 25, 2010.

73 *How America's Faith Has Changed Since 9-11,* Barna Research Online, 2001-Nov-6, at *http://www.barna.org/cgi-bin/.* Retrieved July 25, 2010.

74 Chuck Colson, *Against the Night: Living in the New Dark Ages.* (Ann Arbor, MI: Servant Publications, 1989). P.44.

75 Geraldine Hankins, *American Legal System is Corrupt Beyond Recognition, Judge Tells Harvard Law School.* At: *http://www.massnews.com*, (March 7, 2003. Retrieved July 20, 2010).

76 ibid

77 ibid

78 David Barton, p. 99.

79 *Public Corruption in the United States.* (Report by: Corporate Crime reported, January 16, 2004. National Press Club. Washington D.C.). p. 2.

80 ibid, p. 3.

81 ibid, p.8.

82 ibid, p.10.

83 Lisa Olsen, *Judging the Judges: Veil of Secrecy Stirring Calls for Change.* Texas (Houston Chronicle, Thursday, December 31, 2009).

84 ibid

85 ibid

86 Geoffrey P. Miller, *Bad Judges.* (Texas Law Review, vol. 83:431. Available at: *http://www.utexas.edu/../miller.pdf*) Retrieved July 29, 2010. p.6.

87 ibid

88 ibid

89 ibid

90 ibid

91 ibid

92 ibid

93 ibid

94 Geraldine Hawkins, op.cit.

95 *I Peter* 4:17 (NIV)

96 Transcript: *Interview with Jessica Hahn.* (Larry King Live. CNN. 2005-07-14. *http://transcripts.cnn.com/transcripts/0507/14/lkl.01.html*). Retrieved April 17, 2008.

97 Joanne Kaufman, reported by Kent Demaret, Anne Maier, and Joyce Wadler, *The Fall of Jimmy Swaggert.* (*People Magazine*, vol 29, No. 9, March 7, 1988).

98 Ostling, Richard N. (1988-12-10). *Jim Bakker's Crumbling World.* (Time Magazine). Retrieved May 12, 2007.

99 ibid

100 U.S. v. Bakker (C.A.A., 1991), 925 F.2d 728, 740, case no. 89-5687.

101 Pfeifer, Justice Paul E. (April 12, 2000). *Jim Bakker's Federal Court Appeal.* (Supreme Court of Ohio website). Retrieved November 29, 2007.

102 Jay Bakker, *Son of a Preacher Man.* (New York: Harper Collins, 2001. ISBN 0-06-251698-1)

103 Joanne Kaufman. op.cit.

104 Jon Trott and Mike Hertenstein. *Why the Dates Don't Work.* (Cornerstone. Chicago, IL. July 1992, release A, 7 November 1997). Retrieved August 1, 2010.

105 Diane Sawyer, *The Apple of God's Eye.* ABC News, *Primetime Live*, November 21, 1991.

106 *Swaggart Plans to Step Down.* (*New York Times.* 1991-10-15 *http://guery.nytimes.com/gst/fullpage.html?res=9DOCE SDATE3BF936A25753C1A967958260.*

107 Mark Haville, *Giving Their Lives to the Faith.* (Evangelicals Now) Retrieved August 1, 2010.

108 ibid

109 Tim Wyatt, *Evangelist Gets 16 Month Term in Tax Case.* (*Dallas Morning News.* July 23, 1996). Retrieved August 1, 2010.

110 *Feds Indict Lyons, Women.* St Petersburg Times, July 3, 1998).

111 *Tearful Baptist Leader is Given 5 ½ Year Term in Graft Case.* (*New York Times*).

112 Joel Lawson, *Ex Gay Leader Confronted in Gay Bar.* (Southern Voice. September 21, 2000).

113 Philip Jenkins, *Pedophiles and Priests.* (New York: Oxford University Press). p. 50 and 81.

114 Laurie Goodstein, *Decades of Damage; Trail of Pain in Church Crisis Leads to Nearly Every Diocese.* (New York Times, January 12, 2003). Section 1, p.1.

115 Cal Thomas, *Their Sins Only Start With Abuse.* (Baltimore Sun, June 19, 2002). P. 9A.

116 James L. Franklin, *Sexual Misconduct Seen as a Serious Problem in Religion.* (*Boston Globe*, October 23, 1991). P.24.

117 *Pastors are People Too.* (Focus on the Family, May 1996.) p.7.

118 *Assemblies of God Tackles Problem of Porn Addiction Among Ministers.* (Charisma, January 2001). p. 24.

119 Michael Dobie, *Violation of Trust. Newsday*, June 9, 2002). p.C25

120 Ted Olsen, *Former TBN Employee Alleges Gay Tryst with Paul Crouch.* (Christianity Today. September 1, 2004.) Retrieved August 3, 2010.

121 Robert Marus, *Former Southern Baptist Pastor Acquitted of Seeking Gay Sex.* (Baptist Press. March 12, 2007.) Retrieved August 3, 2010.

122 *Pastor of 2nd Colorado Evangelical Church Resigns Over Gay Sex Allegations. (Seattle Times.* December 12, 2006.) Retrieved August 3, 2010.

123 Hovind v. Commissioner, T. C. Memo.2006-143, CCH Dec. 56, 562 (M) (2006). ['] Retrieved August 13, 2010.

124 *Disgraced Pastor Haggard Admits Second Relationship With Man.* (CNN.com/US Larry King, January 29, 2009.) Retrieved August 3, 2010.

125 Norman Jameson, *Moral Activist Privette Arrested.* (Biblical Recorder News. July 20, 2007.) Retrieved August 3, 2010.

126 *Cops: Televangelist Juanita Bynum Assaulted by Husband.* (Associated Press. August 23, 2007. FoxNews.com.) Retrieved August 3, 2010.

127 J. Lee Grady, *It's Time to Blow the Whistle on Corruption. (Charisma Magazine*, October 19, 2007. cited in: *http://en.wikipedia.org/wiki/list_of_Christian-evangelist_scandals*). Retrieved August 3, 2010.

128 *Tulsa County Judge Dismisses Former ORU President Richard Roberts From Students' Lawsuit.* (*Seattle Times*. March 17, 2009.) Retrieved August 3, 2010.
129 Armen Keteyian, *Televangelists Living Like Kings?* (CBSNews.com, November 6, 2007.) Retrieved August 3, 2010.
130 ibid
131 Alex Daniels, *Jet-Setting Pastor Fights U. S. Inquiry, "Didn't Misuse Ministry Fund", he says.* (*Arkansas-Democrat-Gazette*, Little Rock. October 11, 2009.) Retrieved August 3, 2010.
132 Tanya Miserere and Sam Hodges, *Minister at Prestonwood Baptist Charged in Internet Sex Sting.* (Dallas Morning News. May 17, 2008.) Retrieved August 5, 2010.
133 ibid
134 *FBI Agents Raid Arkansas Church in Child Porn Case.* (The Associated Press. KEAL News, Los Angeles, California. CBS. September 21, 2008.) Retrieved August 5, 2010.
135 *Tony Alamo Convicted of Sex Charges.* (United Press International. UPI. Cited at: *http://www.upi.com/topnews/2009/07/24/Tony-Alamo-convicted-of-sex-charges/*. UPI-377412484640651. July 24, 2009.) Retrieved August 5, 2910.
136 Adrienne S. Gaines, *Todd Bentley Remarries, Begins Restoration Process.* (Charisma. March 10, 2009.) Retrieved August 5, 2010.
137 Penn Bullock and Brandon K. Thorp, *Christian Right Leader George Rekers Takes Vacation with "Rent Boy".*
(*Miami New Times*. May 6, 2010.) Retrieved August 5, 2010.

138 *Wife of Televangelist Benny Hinn Files for Divorce.* (The Associated Press. KEAL News, Los Angeles, California. CBS. February 18, 2010.) Retrieved August 5, 2010.

139 The dates of the study were April 5-7, 2002. It was reported in Roper Center at University of Connecticut, *Public Opinion Online*, Accession Number 0402247. (Hart and Teeter Research Companies did the Survey.)

140 *A New Generation Expresses Its Skepticism and Frustration With Christianity.* (The Barna Group, Ltd. 2009. September 24, 2007. cited at:
http://www.barna.org/teens-next-gen-articles/94-a-new-generation-expresses-its-skepticism-....) Retrieved August 1, 2010.

141 ibid

142 ibid

143 NBC Nightly News; May 4, 1999.

144 Compiled by Author from various news reports.

145 ibid

146 ibid

147 Good Morning America. March 15, 1993. Story from the National Weather Service.

148 The Princeton University Geoscience 499 Class, *The Increasing Cost of US Natural Disasters.* (at:
http://www.agiweb.org/geotimes/nov.05/featuredisastercosts.htm.)

149 Carla R. McMillan, *Natural Disasters: Prepare, Mitigate, Manage.* (Released 1998, at:
http://www.csa.com/discoveryguides/archives/ndht.php#earth.

150 *Northridge Earthquake.* (at:
http://nisee.berkley.edu/northridge.) Retrieved June 11, 2011.

151 *Southeastern United States Palm Sunday Tornado Outbreak of March 27, 1994.* (U.S. Department of Commerce. National Oceanic and Atmospheric Administration. National Weather Service, at: *http://www.nws.noaa.gov/om/assessments/pdfs/palmsund ay.pdf.*) Retrieved June 11, 2011.

152 Eric Klinenberg, *Dead Heat: Why Don't Americans Sweat Over Heat Related Deaths.* (Released July 30, 2002, at: *http://www.slate.com/id/20686121.*)

153 ibid

154 *Billion Dollar U.S. Weather Disasters.* (at: *http://webcache,googlevsercontent.com/search?q=cache :2Y9sOd61X7AJ:www.ncdc.noaa.gov/oa/reports/billionz. html.na.*) Retrieved June 11, 2011.

155 ibid

156 *National Geographic* 195, No. 3 (March 1999), p.83, 94.

157 *Billion Dollar U.S. Weather Disasters*, op.cit.

158 ibid

159 ibid

160 ibid

161 USGS, at: *http://www.usgs.gov/hazards.* Retrieved August 5, 2010.

162 *Independent Insurance Agents of America Report.* At: *http://www.inscenter.com/risk-profile. Retrieved August 5, 2010.*

163 Charts: USGS: *Number of Earthquakes in the United States for 2000-2011* and *Earthquake Information for the 1990's.* at: *http://earthquake.usgs.gov/earthquakes/egarchives/year/ egstats.php.* Retrieved June 11, 2011

164 *Tornado Statistics by Year and Month 1950-1997.* at: *http://www.disastercenter.com/tornado/tornadz.htm*

165 *Monthly and Annual US Tornado Summaries.*
NOAA's Weather Service Storm Prediction Center. At:
http://www.spcnoaa.gov/climo/online/monthly/newm.html
166 *Billion Dollar U.S. Weather Disasters.* op.cit.
167 ibid
168 *Epic Disaster: The World's Worst Disasters.* (at:
http://www.epicdisasters.com/index.php/site/comments.
169 *Billion Dollar U.S. Weather Disasters.* op.cit.
170 ibid
171 *2007: Record Year for Disasters.* Disaster News
Network. At:
*http://www.diseasternews.net/news/article.php?articleid
=3578&printthis=1.* Retrieved June 14, 2011.
172 ibid
173 *SPC Storm Report for April 16, 2011.* Storm Prediction Center. 2011-04-17. Retrieved April 17, 2011.
176 Diana Rosenberg, May 18, 2011, *RMS: Insured
Losses from Late April Tornadoes Could Reach $6 Bil-
lion.* (A.M. Best Company Inc.) Retrieved May 20,
2011.
177 Richard Esposito, Leezel Tangalo, Kevin Dolak, and
Michel Murray, May 23, 2011, *90 Dead in Joplin Missouri After Deadliest American Tornado in 60 Years.*
(ABC News.) Retrieved May 23, 2011.
178
*http://www.worldweatherpost.com/2011/05/25/deadly-
tornadoes-rip-ok-ks-and-ar-high-tornado-risk-today-
Joplin-tornado-an-ef-5/.* Retrieved June 14, 2011.
179 *2007: Record Year for Disasters.* op.cit.
180 Rychard Manne, *Why So Many Earthquakes This
Decade?* At:
*http://www.science20.com/florilegium/blog/Why-so-
many-earthquakes-decade-65178.* Retrieved June 16,
2011.

181 *Flight Path Study – American Airlines Flight.* (PDF. National Transportation Safety Board. February 19, 2002.)

182 *Flight Path Study–United Airlines Flight.* (PDF. National Transportation Safety Board. February 19, 2002.)

183 Flight *Path Study – American Airlines Flight 77.* (PDF. National Transportation Safety Board. February 19, 2002.)

184 *Flight Path Study – United Airlines Flight 93.* (PDF. National Transportation Safety Board. February 19, 2002.)

185 *Lost Lives Remembered During 9/11 Ceremony.* (The Online Rocket. September 12, 2008.) Retrieved August 29, 2010.

186 Michael E. Rolince, June 24, 2003, *The Inspector General's Report and the September 11th Response.* (Federal Bureau of Investigation. United States Department of Justice. September 27, 2001) Retrieved June 17, 2011.

187 Dale L. Watson, February 6, 2002, *The Terrorist Threat Confronting the United States.* (Federal Bureau of Investigation. United States Department of Justice. Archived from the original on May 24, 2008.) Retrieved June 17, 2011.

188 *Responsibility for the Terrorist Atrocities in the United States, September 11, 2001.* (10 Downing Street, November 14, 2001. Archived from the original on September 7, 2004.) Retrieved June 17, 2011.

189 1998 Al Qaeda Fatawa. (Fas.org.) Retrieved November 9, 2010.

190 *http://www.washintonpost.com/blogs/ezra-klein/post/the-economics-of-obama-arab-spring-*

speech/2011/05/19/AFlhOK76_blog.html. Retrieved
June 18, 2011.

191 *Demographics of the Arab League*, computed by
Wolfram Alpha at:
*http://www.wolframalpha.com/input/?=arab+league+de
mographics.* Retrieved June 18, 2011.

192 Ben Stein, *Arab Spring is a Fraud.* At:
*http://www.cbsnews.com/stories/2011/05/15/sunday/main
20063017.shtml.* Retrieved June 18, 2011.

193 Daniel Byman and Christine Fair, July/August 2010,
The Case for Calling Them Nitwits. (*The Atlantic Magazine.* (At:
*http://www.theatlantic.com/magazine/archive/2010/07/
the-case-for-calling-them-nitwits/8103/.*) Retrieved June
18, 2011.

194 ibid

195 Katia A., January 11, 2010, *Tademait's Kamikaze
Had Been Raped Before Being Charged With a Mission.*
(At: *http://www.ennaharonline.com/en/news/173.html.*)
Retrieved June 18, 2011.

196 ibid

197 *Military Casualty Information.* (At:
*http://sladapp.dmdc.osd.mil/personnel/CASUALTY/casto
p.htm.*) Retrieved June 18, 2011.

198 *Cost of Iraq, Afghanistan, and Anti-Terrorism Oper-
ations.* (At:
*http://journalistsresource.org/studies/government/intern
ational/cost-iraq-afghanistan-terror/,* Journal-
ist'sresourc.org.) Retrieved June 18, 2011.

199 Greg Miller, May 5, 2011, *CIA Spied on bin Laden
From Safe House.*
(At:*http://washingtonpost.com/world/cia-spied-on-bin-
laden-from-safe-house/2011/05/05/AFXbG31F-story-.*
The Washington Post.) Retrieved June 18, 2011.

200 Joshua Fost, *Osama bin Laden's Death and Its Impact on US Foreign Policy.* (May 14, 2011 at: http.pbs.org/wnet/net-to-know/five-things/osama-bin-ladens-death-and-its-impact-on-u-s-foreign-policy/9057/. Retrieved June18, 2011.

201 ibid

202 ibid

203 *A Year After Iraq War – Mistrust of America in Europe Ever Higher, Muslim Anger Persists.* (Survey report, The Pew Research Center.2004. at: *http://people-press.org/2004/03/16/a-year-after-iraq-wnrl.* Retrieved June 18, 2011.

204 Charles B. Curtis, *Curbing the Demand for Mass Destruction.* September 2006. (The Annals of the American Academy of Political and Social Science, at: *http://www.sagepub.com/martin3study/articles/curtis.pdf.* Retrieved June 18, 2011.

205 ibid

206 ibid

207 Ben Stein, op.cit.

208 *IAEA Inspectors Found Traces of Highly Enriched Uranium in Iran.* (Regnum. 2006.) Retrieved June 19, 2011.

209 *Exclusive: Iran Says Nuclear Fuel Production Goes Very Well.* (Reuters, Tehran at: *http://www.reuters.com/article/2010/02/11/us-iran-nuclear-salehi-idUSTRE61A4AS20100211.* Retrieved June 19, 2011.

210 Catherine Philip, February 11, 2010, *Mahmoud Ahmadinejad Declares Iran a "Nuclear State" After Producing Enriched Uranium.* (London: The Times.) Retrieved February 11, 2010.

211 *Exclusive: Iran Says Nuclear Fuel Production Goes Well.* op.cit.

212 David Barton, op.cit.

213 Bill Bright, op.cit. p.194

214 ibid

215 ibid

216 ibid

217 ibid

218 John 14:6 (NIV)

219 Acts 4:12 (NIV)

220 John 14:6 (NIV)

221 The Cold War Museum. *Journal of Cold War Studies: The Fall of the Soviet Union.* (at: *http://www.coldwar.org/articles/90s/fall-of-the-soviet-union.asp.* Retrieved June 23, 2011.

222 Timelines, *USSR.* (At: http//www.timelinesolb.com See May 1, 1990.) Retrieved June 23, 2011.

223 *A Christian Martyr Every 5 Minutes.* (*The Church of England Newspaper.* June 17, 2011. p.1. at: *http://geoconger.wordpress.com/2011/06/22/a-christian-martyr-every-5-minutes-the-church-of-england-newspaper-June-17-2011-p-1/*)

224 Dr. Bob Moorehead, *The Fellowship of the Unashamed: The Words Aptly Spoken* (December 1995, at: *http://www.toddtyszka.com/unshamed.html.*) Retrieved June 23, 2011.